Many of us long for more loving and
Many of us long for a more loving and harmonious world.

Creating Harmony shares an engaging and compelling vision of how we can create better lives and a better world.

This book is about a discovery of parts to a whole. The whole is what we can call an aligned action. It's a discovery of functional common denominators between body parts and behaviors. By comparing behaviors to body parts, in terms of their functions, it gives us a way to see and know what is required for alignment in our lives and world.

When we step back and look at the body, we see a whole that we can agree is made up of parts—functioning parts. When we step back and look at an aligned action, similarly, we can see a whole, a harmonious whole, made up of parts — functioning parts: behavioral functioning parts.

But we haven't recognized what they are. There are particular parts to an aligned action, for wholeness, just as clear as there are particular parts to a body, for wholeness. Being *loving* (a functioning behavior) is like the heart in a functional way. Being *thoughtful* (a functioning behavior) is like the brain in a functional way, being *responsive* is like the nerve in a functional way, and so on.

Behaviors, such as being thoughtful and being responsive and several others come together as a whole, aligned act.

In this book, we look at nine essential behaviors and four shared needs that are essential to harmony, based on a functional discovery of how parts relate to wholes. If we step back and look at harmony, it's wholeness.

Published by ThinkLoveAct.com, LLC Madison, Connecticut.

DEDICATION

To Matthew, Tyler and Christopher

Contents

Introduction

INTRODUCTION

Our Gifts

We can share in more truly happy and harmonious lives. We can heal the imbalances in our relationships. More peace and balance is within our reach. Individually and collectively, we can build a world reflective of true happiness, freedom, life, and equality for all.

We say this because there is a discovery being offered here about the workings of nature, and how harmony can be created.

Our heart is a symbol of being loving. Our brain is a symbol of being thoughtful. Our nerves are a symbol of being responsive. But these associations between heart and love, brain and thoughtfulness, and nerves and responsiveness are more than symbols. There is an underlying function that is in common between the heart and love, between the brain and thoughtfulness, and between the nerves and responsiveness. Being loving and the heart share, in common, the function of pumping (giving and receiving). In common between being thoughtful and the brain is the function of processing. In common between being responsive and the nerves is the function of responding. These functional commonalities are critical to understanding how this is a discovery about creating harmony.

These commonalities can guide us. For example, just as the heart is central and connected to the whole system (our body), love is central and connected to the wholeness of our lives and relationships. The heart pumps blood with nourishing resources. Similarly, we can say that being loving involves pumping nourishing resources, such as time, attention, affection.

CREATING HARMONY

If we want to learn to be more loving, or if we want to teach others how to be more loving, we can focus on looking at how we devote our time, attention, affection and other resources — how we pump, how we give and receive. But this is not all. When we see how being loving, in the sense we have just described, is connected to other parts, like being thoughtful and being responsive, we start to get a picture that love, thoughtfulness, and responsiveness are powerful tools, and parts, for creating harmony, much as the heart, brain, and nerves are powerful "tools," and parts, in the body for creating physiological harmony. Furthermore, from this correlation we learn more about what it means to be loving, what it means to be thoughtful, and what it means to be responsive.

The tendency is to not to think about these words, these concepts, themselves. We might think of the idea of "random acts of kindness" or "be curious not furious," or "life is good," but we don't dig into the words *loving, thoughtful, responsive*. But when we do, understanding them as parts, and as functioning parts, at that, we can diagnose ourselves to see if our love is behaving like a healthy heart, to see if our thought is behaving like a healthy brain, to see if our responses are behaving like a healthy nerve.

This is what we explore. What is love? What is thoughtfulness? What is responsiveness? And what are the other parts of whole, harmonious action, and how do they fit together for creating aligned actions, and harmony in our relationships and lives — and world. In the end, we find that there is a discovery here.

The discovery is: being loving is one part of wholeness, serving a particular function which acts like the heart; being thoughtful is one part of wholeness, serving a particular function which acts like the brain; being responsive is one part of

INTRODUCTION

wholeness, serving a particular function which acts like the nerves. Those behaviors, being loving, thoughtful, responsive and each of several other behavioral parts helps to create harmonious, aligned actions. Harmonious, aligned action may, itself, not be a very clear idea. As we go, we'll see what we mean by such a seemingly nebulous, or difficult to define concept, one which, nonetheless, has an intuitive appeal, one which we feel we know it when we see it, but we couldn't necessarily define for others, or for ourselves for that matter. Does it have to do with building a better life? Or, does it have to do with creating more broadly shared harmony? Or both?

Beyond looking at the meaning of behaviors, such as those mentioned, thus far, to recognize the meaning of harmony we must look at values. This is, also in part, a discovery about a very unique relationship between behaviors and *values*. There are certain values that are essential to wholeness and alignment. These, too, share a functional common denominator with particular parts of the body. The values of life (along with life's essentials), liberty, happiness, and equality, as written about, as being self-evident rights, in the U.S. Declaration of Independence, share something in common with the cell, lungs, enzymes and veins, important parts in the body. What is the function of the cell? Do life's essentials, such as food, water and shelter play a similar functional role in our lives? What is the function of lungs? Does liberty, or freedom, play a similar role in our lives? And if so, if there are similarities, does it suggest that life, or life's essentials, and liberty are critical elements for whole, aligned action — and harmony — much as the cell and lungs are critical for physiological wholeness? This is what we are exploring and putting to the test.

CREATING HARMONY

Life, liberty, happiness and equality are values that, again, one might intuitively recognize as being essential to harmony and balance in relationships, but ones which we might not give a second thought. We probably all agree some amount of freedom is important. We also agree that life, and life's essentials are important. And we agree that some amount of happiness is important. And, we probably all want to be treated as equals. But beyond believing that these are values which we hold dear, by recognizing what these have in common with parts of the body, we are able to justify — and better understand — their role, what they mean and why they are essential to wholeness.

The parts of the body which serve similar functions as these values (life and the cell, liberty and lungs, happiness and enzyme, equality and veins) are not as easily or intuitively connected as, for example, love and the heart, but, nonetheless, logically connected. It is, one might say, a fascinating possibility that we, as a society, are developing—and valuing—behaviors and values which align with parts of the body. It is as if as society gets better at displaying these behaviors, and realizing these values, we are developing in the image of the body.

1

The Functional Insight

CREATING HARMONY

The value of simile, metaphor and analogy

It's not easy to think about how love is like the heart, or thoughtfulness is like the brain, or why that matters. But it matters because for us to suggest that for wholeness to be achieved we need to bring several behaviors and values together, we must have some way to support such an assertion. And this is where the comparison to the workings of the body is important.

To understand this better, we can first start by doing some basic review of the value of similes, analogies and metaphors. Comparisons of the *body* to *action, heart* to *love, brain* to *thought, nerves* to *response, cell to life* will, in the end, broaden our understanding of how we might create more wholeness in our lives and society.

Comparisons can help us understand difficult concepts more easily. We use one particular to understand a very different particular. For example, the simile *love is like a rose* helps us to understand love, because the similarity alluded to, between love and a rose, is that both are beautiful. We, certainly, might know that about love, but hearing it compared that way strengthens our association of love with beauty. So, a simile compares two dissimilar things to create a better understanding of the one of the two which is less clear, or otherwise hard to understand. What is love? Love is like chocolate. Again, it has the same effect. It's suggestive that both are enjoyable. Alternatively, to say, love is like a roller coaster conveys an obvious point, that some people might have, that love has its ups and downs. None of these comparisons are perhaps that revealing, and they are also very subjective. They're trying to help define love, but they are subject to opinion and different points of view. A more concrete and objective comparison, however, can provide important insight. A famous analogy is that of the apple to the moon in Newton's Law of Gravity. He observes the apple falling to the ground and knows it does so because of gravity and wonders if that is what holds the moon in orbit. The idea he posits is that if an apple is shot out of a canon, it will travel above the surface of the earth, until it falls, and he suggests that this is what is happening with the moon. The moon is, unlike the apple which is only temporarily in motion above the earth, in constant motion above the earth, and it is constantly held in orbit. So, he analogizes the apple to the moon to show some similarities, though there are differences. He uses one particular to understand a very different particular, to gain a clearer understanding of the moon's action, and how gravity acts upon the moon. If not for some force pulling the moon down it would keep sailing out away from the earth. That's the meaning and value of making similes and analogies.

By contrast to a simile and analogy, Shakespeare's "All the world's a stage, and all the men and women merely players. They have their exits and their entrances" is a metaphor. The world is not a stage. But it seems like a stage, at least, so says Shakespeare. The lesson gleaned there from the metaphor is that we might see our lives as being part of a play, and we might see ourselves as playing roles in that play. And in so doing, we might, for example, take ourselves less seriously, perhaps. So, we learn a little from the metaphor too, as we did with similes and analogies. Each of these forms of comparison have value. And to some degree we take that for granted and don't likely give much thought to the device.

Where the device has powerful value, here, is to show that we can "piece together" (or use) "parts" (or behaviors and values) for harmony. The comparison between two spheres, the body and the

CREATING HARMONY

behavioral, is extremely revealing. It reveals a hidden insight into harmony. It sheds light on how we might improve our ability to create harmony.

Let's begin to explain with one of the behaviors, meaningfulness. The concept of meaningfulness from an intuitive place we might say likely relates to creating fulfilling lives, and perhaps, harmonious lives. Even without an analogy we recognize the concept or behavior of meaningfulness as being valuable. In other words, it's important to have meaning in our lives, or for them to be meaningful, most would agree.

But now, let's make a comparison to deepen or further our understanding of the essential role of meaningfulness for creating harmony. If we say "meaning is like the muscles, it moves us and people," we're using a simile and explaining the simile ("it moves us and people")—we're explaining the relationship. We don't generally think of meaningfulness in terms of creating movement. Yet, both the muscles and acting with meaning, do, in fact, create movement. It's easy to see how muscles create movement. It's harder to see how meaningfulness does, but once explained it becomes clear: For example, a poem or a song that is meaningful to a person moves them emotionally. A product that makes our lives easier is meaningful because it gets something important done—in the process it creates movement.

Some products, we may not think of as creating movement, though we may recognize that they are meaningful. Yet all products, in one way or another, do create movement. For example, we may not think of a refrigerator as creating movement, yet we recognize it is meaningful, or important. But it does create movement, and it is the movement that it creates that relates to its meaning. It makes or moves the temperature of items in it to the point where they are cold and thereby preserves them.

THE FUNCTIONAL INSIGHT

It's not the type of movement we may think of as movement, generally, but it is a movement which matters. This may be an obscure way of understanding a product, or by extension products, and our world, but it is nonetheless a valuable approach. Imagine a refrigerator that only moves the temperature to fifty degrees, then imagine one that moves the temperature to forty degrees. The one that matters, the one that is more valuable, is the one that moves the temperature more. Consider a different example. A laptop is meaningful. We may not think of the meaningfulness of the laptop in terms of what it moves, but we can. We can think of it as moving letters and ideas ... The better, faster, more powerfully it moves, and the more valuable the content it moves, the more meaningful the product, itself, is.

Now, let's look more closely at the comparison between meaningfulness and the muscles. If we say, "meaning is a muscle," we're using a metaphor—and that's sounds awkward—meaning is a muscle? That's like saying the apple is a moon. But when we explain the comparison, naturally, we better understand it. We can say the action of an apple, shot out of a canon, shed light on the action of the moon, in that they both are affected by gravity. We learn from the comparison. Here, when we compare meaningfulness to muscles what we are saying is that acting meaningfully creates movement much as the muscles create movement. The extension of that is that we might adopt the idea that, when we are trying to make our lives more meaningful, we might want to try to create more constructive, productive *movement*. For example, the couch potato is not meaningful, living vicariously is not as meaningful as making or producing or creating something — all things made, produced or created produce movement; again we are suggesting we want to make constructive, productive movement. This is where, as we go along, we see how other behaviors work together with being meaningful. So, thoughtful products, caring products, create *constructive* movement. Whereas, thoughtless, uncaring products create movement, but arguably, not valuable or meaningful movement: a destructive act is often, called senseless, or meaningless. Just like we recognize that a brain, a heart … makes a whole person, we can recognize that key behaviors and values, or parts, make a whole, harmonious action.

It is not only the idea that there are parts to whole, harmonious actions that we are trying to convey, we are also trying to convey the idea that we can learn that behaviors serve functions. Meaningfulness serves the function of creating movement.

Further, we are trying to convey that we can learn from the comparison of the body how to foster behaviors, such as meaningfulness, by recognizing how the body works. For example, we develop muscles, and they work, by stretching and repetition, resisting force. So, too, we can improve our ability to act meaningfully, by stretching and repetition, resisting force by working through challenges. For example, we know that we develop our ability to communicate (one activity which creates movement) meaningfully when we practice telling and retelling (or stretching and repeating, against the tendency toward status quo and undeveloped capabilities) something until it becomes more and more moving, or until it makes more of difference, or is more valuable for people's lives.

Continuing on, we'll take a look at comparisons of several behaviors and values to several different organs in our body. We'll look further at *muscles* and *meaning*, and we'll look at *tendons* and *uniting*, *nerves* and *responding* and several others. The analogy between muscles and meaning is not to say that we want to develop better bodies, better physical beingness, no more than Newton was saying that the moon ought to behave like an apple. No, he simply said, maybe they actually do behave like each other for a reason, in terms of gravity. The moon lights up the sky at night, the apple gets eaten. They're not alike in all ways. But by recognizing where they are alike we can learn something about something we did not otherwise know or understand. When we look at functions of particular parts of the body, we see that they have value for making the whole body work. So too, when we look at particular behaviors, such as acting meaningfully or responsively, we see that they have value for making an interaction whole, balanced and harmonious, and by extension our lives, whole, balanced and harmonious.

What the body informs is that much as the muscles, brain, nerves, cells, and several other body parts, when healthy, come together for a physiological whole body, several behaviors, like meaningfulness, thoughtfulness, responsiveness, and several values, like life's essentials, liberty, happiness and equality, can come together for wholeness and harmony in our lives and societies.

2

Body and Behavior?

BODY AND BEHAVIOR?

Imagine the physical body as one layer of our experience. Imagine the behaviors and values that we exhibit as being another layer of experience that is embedded in the physical body and that affects the world around us.

To better understand how each of the important behaviors and values relates to parts of the body, and to harmonizing lives and societies, we're going to look more closely at analogies, and their related cousins, similes and metaphors. What we'll see is how these comparisons reveal a functional discovery. Much as Newton's law of gravity was a formula of sorts, so too, this discovery is of a formula, or law of nature of sorts.

What exactly is an analogy?

Put aside Newton's "apple is to moon," and let's look at a different analogy to help explain the behavioral analogy to the body.

Plant: Forest:: _____ : House.

a. home
b. cozy
c. roof

Hint: "The relationship between the first pair of words is that of part to whole—one word is a part or piece of the other."[1]

So, the answer to this is c, roof. Plant is a part of a forest and a roof is a part of a house. However, what's slightly tricky about that example is that roof is part of house but it seems out of line with plant and forest because plant sits at the bottom of a forest and the roof sits at the top of a house. Also, the roof is seemingly structurally attached for a particular purpose to the house, while plants are not so clearly attached for a purpose to the forest. Nonetheless, the reality with analogy, in general, is that there are similarities between items being compared, but there are also differences. To better see why we are comparing behaviors to body parts, let's look more at how the analogies come together for wholeness.

Let's begin with this idea:

> Plant is to Forest as Muscles are to Body

That's obvious - parts to a whole.

Less obvious:

> Plant is to Forest as Meaningfulness is to Whole, Aligned Action

That's far less obvious. We simply do not think of any particular behavior as having any specific relationship to whole, aligned action. We could refer to kindness, caring, tolerance, any number of behaviors, and suggest they, too, are part of whole, aligned action. So, why do we pick specific behaviors? As we've been explaining to this point, we pick behaviors that align in some ways with the function of body organs.

Instead of saying *Plant is to Forest* as Muscles are to Body, what we're saying is:

BODY AND BEHAVIOR?

Meaningfulness is to Whole, Aligned Action as *Muscles are to Body.*
Responsiveness is to Whole, Aligned Action as *Nerves are to Body.*

That is, again, parts to a whole, but it's a little more. We're actually offering another layer of analogy. In the above original analogy, Plant is to Forest as Muscles are to Body, plant and muscles are not related, except that they're both pieces to a whole, in no other way are they similar. Plant is to Forest as Muscles are to Body, or as Roof is to House, is making one point and only one point, that they are parts to a whole. A rather meaningless analogy. If, instead of saying *Plant is to Forest as Roof is to House*, we said, "*Plant is to Forest as Floor is to House*," we might notice that there is the further commonality that the plant is at the base of the forest much as the floor is at the base of the house. That is what we are doing when we say *Muscles are to body as Meaningfulness is to Whole, Aligned action*—we're saying that muscles and meaningfulness relate to each other in an important way besides that they are parts of a whole.

What this does is open up some real possibilities for learning and growth. If muscles are similar to meaningfulness, in that they both provide movement, and strong or weak movement, at that, then it is possible that we can learn how to create strong movement in our actions, much as we create strong movement with our bodies. We can learn to develop our meaningfulness, by stretching and by repetitive effort against resistance — practice, practice, practice against our own tendency toward leisure or inaction, or in the face of fear or anxieties that we might have. To get better at any activity, we must practice, or work, against these and other forces. Practicing, working, we are developing our ability to meaningfully contribute. This is true, in an easily explained way, with writing, where we write and re-write (practicing) against resistance. Writing over and over again, we get better and convey more meaningfully.

So, we can develop our ability to act meaningfully by stretching and repetition, and working against counterforces, or weight, the way we develop muscles.

In summary, when we look at each of several behaviors and values in terms of a comparison to the body, we're stringing together a series of comparisons:

Muscles are to the Body as Meaningfulness is to Whole, Aligned Action, in that they both create constructive movement.

Nerves are to the Body as Responsiveness is to Whole, Aligned Action, in that they both respond or signal well.

Senses are to the Body as Sensitivity is to Whole, Aligned Action, in that they both sense, or detect, well.

Tendons are to the Body as Uniting is to Whole, Aligned Action, in that they both unite, or connect, well.

Bones are to the Body as Individualizing is to Whole, Aligned Action, in that they both provide structural support.

BODY AND BEHAVIOR?

Lungs are to the Body as Freedom is to Whole, Aligned Action, in that they both give us the ability to voice and breathe well.

We're stringing together those comparisons and several others.

By way of these comparisons, we're explaining functional common denominators between the two realms, the behavioral and values realm and the body, or physiological, realm. The example we've done so far: moving is the function in common with both muscles and meaningfulness. Something is meaningful when it moves us. So, too, a muscle moves us. Weak muscles move us weakly. Things that are weakly meaningful hardly move us at all. Things that are strong in meaning move us well.

Another example, what does responsiveness have in common with nerves? Responding, or signaling.

Responding, or signaling, is common to responsiveness and to nerves. When we're responsive to others, we're responding, or signaling. When our nerves act, they're responding, or signaling. We can respond defensively or courageously in our behavior. Similarly, our nerves can respond protectively or affirmatively.

Each of these behaviors and values has a function in common with body parts.

Responding, or signaling, is common to responsiveness and nerves.
Sensing, or detecting, is common to sensitivity and senses.
Uniting, or connecting, is common to uniting and tendons.
Distributing is common to equality and the veins.

CREATING HARMONY

The point is that responding, sensing, uniting, distributing... are functional common denominators to behaviors and values and parts of the body.

It is the common shared function that leads to the link between the body organ and the behavior or value. It is the common shared function that leads to the selection of each behavior and value.

Meaningfulness, responsiveness, sensitivity..., each of those relates to specific body parts, and they come together to create a harmonious whole, aligned action.

As for the analogy between being loving and the heart: Pumping, or giving and receiving, is common to loving behavior and the heart. The heart pumps (gives and receives) to and from all parts of the body. With our love, we give and receive to one another. A strong love, a strong heart, gives and receives well.

If you have a weak physical heart, this analogy is not saying it is because you are not loving. If you have a strong heart, this analogy is not saying you are being loving. However, this analogy is saying that, if you want to be more loving, pump, give and receive, to one another the way your heart gives and receives unselfishly, rhythmically and repeatedly to and from all the parts of your body.

3

A Law of Nature

CREATING HARMONY

The comparison of behaviors and values to body parts gives us a clearer picture of the value of behaviors and values. We know what moving, wholeness, pumping (giving and receiving, to and from) look like in a physical realm. The value of something tangible is that it can help us understand something intangible.

So, what we really need to say, at this point, is that this book is not really about an analogy, simile and metaphor so much as it is about something fundamentally different. It's about commonality and variety. It's about what is in common between very different things. Muscles move, but so does meaningfulness. The body is whole, but so is aligned action. The heart pumps, but so does love (and love also moves us, when it is meaningful; the heart is also a muscle).

At the root of the approach is commonality with variety. We can create more love by recognizing this. This is sometimes called a system's insight. But, it's really an insight into nature.

Let's return to Newton. He defined a law of nature. Gravity. It applied to an apple, it applied to the moon, it applied to the universe. This book is defining what may be a law of nature. It's saying moving, wholeness, pumping, these are things that apply to everything, every interaction.[2] In the realization of the commonality and variety, we can create harmony.

Commonality and variety is not implying sameness. It's implying an underlying sameness that branches off and expands through variety. We can create a better world in the commonality and variety. What's true beauty? Is it the cover girl, the football player? It's aligned action, when each of us come to wholeness in our actions moment to moment—through the understanding that we share a make-up for wholeness and oneness and harmony. We share a make-up for Love. And, in understanding and embracing that make-up, we can align our government, our business, our lives. The world is actually moving in this direction of more aligned institutions and lives.

Alignment applies to the way we interact. And, as we are exploring it, it can be validated by logic, common sense and intuition. In the next chapter, we suggest four shared needs. Evaluate for yourself whether the four needs we offer are truly shared and universal.

Universals, those things that we agree upon, are hard to find, but there are some, time is money, life is a journey, these are metaphors that have universal appeal, although they may not have much value for guiding us to make a better world, and they may be debated. Here, we can ask, is it logical, common sense, and intuitive to say that meaningfulness moves people? Is it logical, common sense and intuitive to say muscles move us? Is it logical, common sense and intuitive to say meaningfulness is like the muscles in that sense? Is it logical, common sense, and intuitive to say that love gives and receives to and from people? Is it logical, common sense and intuitive to say the heart gives and receive, to and from, parts of the body? Is it logical, common sense and intuitive to say love is like the heart in that sense? If you can say yes to these questions and the alignments that are developed in the book, then it's logical that these can have value for creating better lives and a better world.

By creating a categorization of behaviors and values, we can better understand how to create harmony. Categorizations are often useful. For example, we can describe classifications of species, genus, family... phylum, and kingdom up to the classification life. So, too, we can classify, or categorize, our behaviors and values. Using those which mimic the human body provides us a guide for "ordering" and "organizing" a set of

CREATING HARMONY

behaviors and values while anchoring them in a system, the body, that exhibits harmonious union and balanced growth.

Prior to Newton, white light was thought to be clear. Newton discovered that white light was made of colors. Through a prism of wholeness, the several behaviors, action, love, thoughtfulness, responsiveness, uniting, individuality, sensitivity, meaningfulness, and empathy, and the several values, life, liberty, happiness and equality show themselves as separate, but they come together as whole, aligned action.

4

Balancing Tensions, Reconciling Differences

CREATING HARMONY

To understand harmony, we have to consider conflict. A simple and rather mundane example helps make the point. Two children have one bicycle between them, and no other toys. This might lead to a conflict. What trying to harmonize or align is doing is trying to resolve or eliminate tensions. In our daily lives, the tensions range from being there in subtle ways, being sometimes brushed under the rug, to, at the other end of the spectrum, being there in pronounced and noticeable ways which may surface as volatility or hostility, as two examples of consequences.

So, how, in the world, is it possible to suggest that the body is a model for creating behavioral, whole, aligned actions, if we have no way to capture all the possible tensions that might exist between people which would need to be harmonized?

Does it really say enough to say be responsive, be meaningful, be thoughtful? It does if we recognize that we want to be responsive, thoughtful ... of the four values of life, liberty, happiness and equality. By returning to the example where we have one bicycle between two children, we can see this in a rudimentary way, to help us understand the methodology and its broader application. It may seem simplistic, but we can actually conceive of that challenge, and all challenges, in terms of four basic values. One or more of these four values arise in every situation of conflict or tension, where "harmonizing" or "aligning" really matters, and can help. With the bicycle, the value of *equality* is what guides us to share — that is, if a child shares the bike it is because he or she should treat another as an equal. Certainly, the child is *free* (the liberty value) to use the bicycle and ignore the other child's desire to ride too, but if he does so, then he may have a conflict that leads to dissatisfaction. Equality is one universal value, as is liberty, and there is often a tension between the two, which has to be reconciled. This is a simplified way of explaining the tension, which will be developed in much more detail for more accuracy, and deeper understanding, but the point here is simply to illustrate the idea.

Also, *happiness* is often in tension with having a *life's essential*. As another simplistic example, but one which is representative of a much more pervasive reality that extends beyond this example, we may pursue having dessert for happiness, but we must balance it with eating healthy food, a life's essential. This is a metaphor for a lot of life. We are constantly making trade-offs, for example, between watching more television (or engaging in a leisure activity) and getting our work done. We must balance meeting our life's essential needs with meeting our happiness objectives.

And so, how do we balance these needs? Well, with the behaviors we've been offering: with meaningfulness, responsiveness, thoughtfulness, uniting… and so on. After all, we need some guiding values to guide our behaviors to because without guiding principles what may seem meaningful to one may not be meaningful to another, what may be thoughtful or responsive to one, may not be thoughtful or responsive to another. Moving into alignment within ourselves and with one another requires that we be responsive to life, liberty, happiness and equality, what we term "our shared universal needs." One can be a nice or not so nice doctor, at times, a nice or not so nice father or mother, at times. What makes for a nice, good, loving action …? It may be that it—the activity, the choice, the decision—meets particular universal values, and has particular behaviors.

We can think of uniting for shared values, we can think of individualizing for shared values, we can think of sensitivity for shared values…

KEY BEHAVIORS

Function	Body	Behavior
Aligning	Whole body	Action
Pumping	Heart	Love
Thinking/ Processing	Brain	Thoughtful
Responding/ Signaling	Nerves	Responsive
Uniting/ Connecting	Tendons	Uniting
Individualizing/ Supporting	Bones	Individualizing
Sensing/ Detecting	Senses	Sensitivity
Moving/ Strengthening	Muscles	Meaningful
Energizing	Emotions	Empathy

5

Acting Aligned

"How wonderful it is that nobody need wait a single moment before starting to improve the world."

- Anne Frank

ACTING ALIGNED

Body part: The whole body (for aligning)

A harmonious, or aligned, action is like an aligned body,
in that they are both wholes made up of parts.

Acting in alignment is a way to describe this idea of bringing behaviors together for harmony. Aligned actions bring together love, thoughtfulness, responsiveness, uniting, individualizing, sensitivity, meaningfulness, empathy, and a whole host of other beautiful behaviors and values. Said differently, aligned action is the manifestation of all the "parts" coming together. Just as a healthy body has parts which together create balance and harmony, so, too, a healthy and aligned action has parts which together create balance and harmony.

Naturally, we might recognize that acting aligned, aligning well within ourselves and with others, is related to being loving and feeling loved. And that when we act out of balance we create disharmony for ourselves and others. We can see the unhealthy effects of imbalance in personal relations, work relations and world relations.

As we've noted, beyond thinking about harmony as being associated with concepts, such as balance, alignment and being loving, we can think about harmony in terms of the values of life's essentials, freedom, equality and happiness.

Most of us would likely agree, we experience some sense of harmony, in the sense that we feel better, when our essential needs for food, water and shelter are met, while at the same time those whom we are with have those needs met as well; and when we are happy, and those whom we are with are happy too; and when we are free and equal and those whom we are with also feel they are free and treated equally. This is why we can think of these values as being necessary parts of alignment, or balance. The idea that we are aligned when we have all four of these values met, and when we are exhibiting behaviors such as love, thoughtfulness, and responsiveness and so on is a different notion than one which says we must meet one of these essential needs, and then as we grow and get older meet another and another. That is, this approach is saying we can meet each of these in a single interaction, or action.

By contrast, the psychologist, Abraham Maslow, speaks of the idea of a hierarchy, which we might think of as climbing up a ladder. At the bottom we seek to satisfy our basic needs. In the middle, we seek to connect with others with self-esteem and love. And even higher on this path to self-actualization and transcendence is connecting with others and their needs, which is why Martin Luther King, Jr., Mahatma Gandhi, Helen Keller, Jonas Salk and those who have done great things for humanity are offered as examples of this complete, or whole, or superior self, this self which is clearly connected with the well-being of others.

We, many of us, tend to think that we can't achieve what those great figures achieved, and yet, what the alignment model we are considering is suggesting is that we can "align for harmony" in a single interaction. And in so doing we are fully actualizing. And we can do it over and over and over again, one interaction at a time, until, over time, our life reflects a considerable contribution.

But it takes a broadening of our understanding of how the values of life, liberty, happiness and equality relate to even our everyday choices and decisions.

ACTING ALIGNED

And the only way we can become more aware of how they relate is for us to become more thoughtful, responsive, sensitive... to each of these four values. As we do so, we become increasingly aware of how they affect our daily lives and the lives of others.

These values, again, are what the greatest among us worked toward bringing about for the greatest number. They did this with large challenges. We, all of us, have daily opportunities to align our actions, and to make strides to creating better lives and a better world.

How do we get to this state? We build it. We bring the pieces together. We begin to "diagnose" our actions with the objectives of healing and healthy growth.

When we think in terms of parts to alignment, we begin to recognize:

The power of our love to give and receive, giving and receiving in nourishing ways like the heart pumping;

The creative capability of our thought, processing like the brain's memory, storage and computing;

The courage of our right response, responding like the nerves signaling to direct us;

The strength and versatility gained from our ability to unite, connecting like the tendons to give flexibility to our physical structure for a wide range of movement;

The integrity that comes with being our best selves, giving structural support to our lives the way the bones do so for our bodies;

The perceptivity of our sensitivity to guide us, sensing like the senses;

The power and strength of acting meaningfully, powering our lives the way the muscles power our bodies;

CREATING HARMONY

And, the emotive power of expressing empathy to positively energize ourselves and others, energizing like the emotions create movement for the body.

Being aligned means putting together the different capabilities of love, thoughtfulness, responsiveness, uniting, individualizing, sensitivity, meaningfulness, and empathy in a single conversation, in a single meeting, in a single phone call, in a single work day....It means recognizing that we can obtain for ourselves and others life's essentials, happiness, equality and freedom.

6

Being Loving

"It is only with the heart that one can see rightly; what is essential is invisible to the eye."

- Antoine de Saint Exupery (Author)

CREATING HARMONY

Body part: Heart (for linking and for pumping resources to the whole body)

Heart is to the Body

as Being Loving is to Harmonious Action,

in that both, the heart and being loving, involve pumping, or giving and receiving, nourishing resources.

The heart is a symbol of love ♥, and rightly so, as we see what the heart does in our body: pumping resources throughout our whole body, the heart gives and receives continuously.[3] So, too, being loving, we share resources, we give of ourselves and receive from others, acting to nourish.

Giving and receiving resources in a way that is loving means giving and receiving not only material resources, but also things such as constructive, caring and kind words, a warm smile, anything that nourishes life. If it is true, as many suggest, that getting material things doesn't lead to happiness and fulfillment, then we might spend more time learning how to give and receive in these and other non-material ways. Perhaps, one of the most important ways to give and receive is in communication. There, clearly, we can give and receive with love – and most of us can learn to do so more lovingly.

We all can probably make our conversations more caring and nourishing. A simple way is to speak in ways that lift others up. A kind word at the right time, a reassuring comment, an encouraging word for someone who is feeling discouraged, each of these can uplift.

BEING LOVING

Another way to make our conversation more caring is to take an interest in what another wants to share. This is receiving in a way that is giving. Listening to the story another wants to tell or the issue that burdens a person can make another feel loved. It is said that the best conversationalist is the one who listens.

Of course, not everything that a person wants to talk about is healthy and constructive, and so it is caring to be careful not to engage in those conversations which are separating or diminishing. Put downs, criticisms in judgment, these both have negative consequences, and so, require us to guide the conversation higher. Our job is to raise up unhealthy conversations.

Much as caring words are nourishing, caring activities are also nourishing. Working to provide for life's essentials is a caring activity, as is working to make a world that is more equal, free and safe.

Since love is a voluminous topic it is impossible to do it justice in a couple of pages. What's important to recognize here is the value of thinking of love as being about pumping time, attention, affection and resources. We can explore this idea. A starting point is thinking about pumping, and the heart.

Since the heart is, in part, a muscle, we might, first, suggest that pumping requires stretching and repetition, against resistance. We improve our ability to be loving, much as we strengthen any muscle, by stretching, and repetitive effort against force or weight: we get better at being loving by stretching and developing our ability to do so, against perhaps a fear, a habitual tendency, a cultural "no" or norm, or against the different things that weigh us down in our life.

This involves giving time, attention and affection to activities, such as reading about love, and talking about love and what it means. In doing so, we are acting like a pump, giving and receiving, giving of our time, and receiving information, attention and affection.

The resistance against weight, or effort, is that it isn't common to do this. We might come home from work and not think to, or want to, have a discussion about what it means to love. Rather, instead, we might put on the television for a laugh or a diversion. Trying a discussion about how to be more loving, often, is a new thing to do, but stretching against force, or the forces against us, including distractions, involves trying new things, being open and attending to areas where we need growth.

Beyond discussions about how to be more loving, we can give our attention to the topic in meditation or contemplation. This requires us to say no to the distractions.

One of the reasons many advocate meditation is that such practices help us to shut out distractions and temptations. In that space, in that contemplation, we may make decisions to commit to healthier habits and practices. If we are having trouble breaking a particular habit, try taking some time to sit in silence and contemplate a different you, a different way of being – visualize a more loving you, a more loved you.

The goal of this silencing of the mind is to help one to open to something vaster than oneself. Those who engage in such contemplation and meditation invariably focus on learning to express compassion or kindness. Naturally, bringing thoughts of compassion and kindness into our minds more often we grow to become more loving. We act on those thoughts, as energy and action follow thought.

Besides conversation and contemplation about being loving, we can think more about what it is that we most need to be giving and receiving. Life's essentials are of course, essential, as are liberty, happiness and equality, as we've said. So, learning to give these to others while balancing our own needs for them is part of learning to love well.

A common challenge for some: We may be responsive to ourselves and our own desires and longings, but not enough to those of others. Or, we may be sensitive to our own feelings and stories, but not enough to those of others. In balancing, we expand beyond the boundaries of our self to include the other.

The more we expand our ambit of concern, the farther our love reaches. With attention to our own desires for happiness and success while also recognizing others' needs equal to our own we express love.

For some, there is the reverse challenge: We may be responsive to another but not enough to ourselves, or sensitive to another but not enough to ourselves. This may work for a time, but it often leads to frustration and resentment.

It's about creating the right balance, or flow, in and out. At the root of our effort to give and receive well is our ability to make things "two way." Much as the giving and receiving, back and forth, to and from the heart is two way, we can make our relationships two way. If we're receiving more than we are giving, we can learn to give more. If we're giving and receiving meaninglessly or thoughtlessly, we can move toward giving and receiving more meaningfully and more thoughtfully.

Are we giving courageously? Are we receiving courageously? Are we giving and receiving in ways that balance people's needs for life's essentials, liberty, equality and happiness? Are we creating a good flow as a society? Are we creating a good flow as an individual? Are we creating a good flow *for* society? Are we creating a good flow for our close relationships?

CREATING HARMONY

We can see the power of this mutual flow in a simple example. In giving guidance to a child, there is a two way flow, in that we sow a seed of mutual love, respect and adoration. For example, by giving a child tools to be their best self, to believe in themselves, and to find their own inner worth and potential, what comes back to us, if not immediately, is a heart full of love.

To improve our ability to create growth in a child, we may have to steer ourselves to give of our time and attention better. For example, we may want to give our children the time and attention they need to help them develop to be their best selves, but then not give attention to moving them away from excessive TV, videos, and gaming. It takes time and effort to steer children to more creative and constructive activities, such as building things, exploring, drawing, and reading more, and to guide their content choices to be healthy ones, ones that utilize their unique gifts. Of course, this is an area that takes strength and attention.

Creating this balance in our partner relationships also takes strength and attention. We can look at those relationships, and life, more generally, as a dance, as much as a journey. The dance requires us to move in step with another—and it requires us to flow with the music of life, its ups and downs—and particularly, with its downs. It requires us to flow when our differing opinions come to the surface, not when it's easy, but when it's difficult. That is the challenge and the prize. To be loving not only in good times but also in trying ones is essential to growing in our practice of love.

As being loving requires a reciprocal flow, we should be aware of how the other affects the flow. Much as two people who want to dance better together need to practice and may even need to take lessons, so too the dance of love requires us to practice and "take lessons." We can—and need to be—learning lessons regularly, as growth requires it, and health requires it. Much as we need to exercise to keep the heart healthy, so too, we need to exercise to keep our love healthy.

And because we are interdependent, which is a healthy balance of dependence and independence, we need the one we are with to be on the same page with the effort to improve the dance. If those we are involved with are not interested in growing in their ability to harmonize, we may need to leave the relationship, after some agonizing. Certainly, we can "love the one we are with"—our family members and spouse, or partner, friends and colleagues, and enemies — but because there is so much to be learned from the process of giving and receiving love, it is essential that we find someone who wants to grow with us in this area.

How we "find" someone to engage with us in a loving journey, if we are not already with someone and want to be is much simpler than you may think. Simply by setting yourself on the mission to become more loving, you will likely attract someone else who is also seeking to do so. Think of it as you would think of any pursuit or interest, and how it leads you to others with a common interest. If you are interested in art, for example, you will likely meet others who are also interested in art. It is the same principle with finding those who care about becoming more loving: If you are making an interest of yours, and an effort, to become more loving, you will likely meet another who is as well. It may lead you to a particular book, and that book, if you are reading it in public, or if you mention it in conversation, may catch the attention of another.... There are any number of scenarios—we know this is quite common.

But, as with any effort, it is common to focus on the work of making the effort rather than to focus on the joy of doing it, and what comes from it. Of course, it's a matter of focus. If we focus on the joy of growing, we feel better in our effort.

So, where do you start? For starters, we can give time and attention to being thoughtful, responsive, uniting and so on.

When we give our time and attention to *thoughts* that are creative, constructive and caring we sow the seeds for love. And we can build upon this.

When we give our time and attention to creating *responses* which are more open, and less defensive when defense is unnecessary, and to creating *responses* which are warm when warmth is called for, which are feeling when feeling is nourishing, which are understanding when understanding is needed, we send out signals of love.

When we give our time and attention to *uniting* with others, combining our strengths, we strengthen the bond of love.

When we give our time and attention to developing our *individuality* to enrich others' lives, we are providing a support structure for love.

And when we give our time and attention to acting *sensitively,* detecting and acknowledging both our own feelings and the feelings of others, we enjoy the feeling of love.

When we give our time and attention to sharing more *meaningfully*, in ways that provide significant and lasting value, we make our love strong and moving.

And when we give our time and attention to putting ourselves in another's shoes, or *empathizing*, we extend our love beyond ourselves, and create more loving energy in the world.

In, merely, guiding our time and attention to developing behaviors which are harmonizing we improve our ability to love and be loved. Perhaps, that was a lot of effort against resistance (to read, to write)—loving effort ☺.

7

Being Thoughtful

"A small group of thoughtful people could change the world. Indeed, it's the only thing that ever has."

- Margaret Mead

CREATING HARMONY

Body part: Brain (for thinking)

Brain is to the Body

as Thoughtfulness is to Harmonious Action,

in that both, the brain and thoughtfulness, involve processing, computing, and the use of memory.

Being thoughtful involves the use of the brain to be caring. The brain uses memory, storage and processing capability to "think" or "give thought." Similarly, thoughtfulness extends our ability to use our memory, storage and processing capability to do something loving. Remembering someone's birthday, we consider to be thoughtful. Thinking of a nice thing to say, we consider to be thoughtful. Thinking of a way to solve a problem someone is having, so too, we think of as thoughtful. When we put our memory and computational processing capability to work to figure out ways to meet our own needs and the needs of others, we are being thoughtful.

Of course, thought is necessary for creating a balance in our lives. Often, people say they may want balance in their life, and they may think it requires balancing work time and family time. Certainly, time is one resource, a factor of being loving, and when we think of balancing work and family time, we are thinking of *how* we use that time, but what if we were to think more deeply about how we use that time by looking at our behaviors and values within that time.

What if balancing our lives really was about balancing our sensitivity to ourselves and to others? If so, we'd have to think,

BEING THOUGHTFUL

(using the behavior of thoughtfulness) about how to be sensitive in a balanced way. And what if balancing our lives required us to balance our individual strengths with the strengths of others? If so, we'd have to think about how to express our individuality while embracing others individuality, thereby uniting. And what if creating a balance in our lives was about balancing our ability to give and receive, again, not only time, but attention, affection, and other resources? If so, it would mean that we need to better think about how to balance our giving and our receiving.

To this end, if we think about creating a balance as involving balancing life, liberty, happiness and equality, four things we all need, at first, it may seem complicated, but it is also enlightening. Think of it this way, if we want to achieve each of these ideals, then we must think about doing so—and also, we'd have to think about *how* to do so. A balanced life, a harmonious relationship, a fulfilling life doesn't happen without some thought. Anything great that you or anyone has achieved took thought. It's no different with creating harmony. It takes thought, caring thought.

Balancing the needs of oneself with the needs of another is needed because the needs of life, liberty, happiness and equality are sometimes, seemingly at odds. We may have to give up some liberty, or freedom, to realize, or experience equality. For example, we may give up the freedom to act in a way that might be annoying to another. We may, for example, give up playing music loudly in recognition of another's equal right not to be interfered with by loud music.

Extending this idea out to the question of freedom of artistic, or sensational, but "rated" expression, we may give this up so as not to expose or exploit others. When a worldly horror happens, such as what happened on 9/11 or in Newtown, we recognize to shut off the television if there is a young child present. Do we do

49

the same with fictional displays of violence or graphic images which may not be well suited for children? These are questions that balance freedom with equality.

When we shut off the display of violence when a child is around we're recognizing the child's need for healthy development as being equal to our own adult need, or longing, for information or entertainment. Apart from that example, there are innumerous examples in our daily lives where our decisions are balancing freedom with equality, and such has benefits for happiness. When, for example, partners share equally in decision-making, giving up some individual liberty, for example, it has been shown that both partners are happier.

How to strike the balance, giving up some freedom, for equal respect and regard, involves personal decisions which require thought. It takes thought to give up what we may think of as an important or pleasurable pursuit, but one which might not be great for another, or even for ourselves.

Often it involves looking at the difference between the short and long-term impacts of a choice. Thinking about the longer-term impacts on ourselves and on others, naturally, we may have to give up some short-term "happiness" in consideration of our own or others' long-term happiness. This, of course, takes some thought, some reflection.

And much as we may have to give up some personal freedom, for either short or long-term happiness, we may have to give up some happiness to meet some of our own or others' essential needs (food, water, shelter...). Many people often forego a desired pleasurable experience to meet a life's essential need. We may forego a vacation, or dinner out, as examples, to afford an essential.

BEING THOUGHTFUL

We may recognize being thoughtful as involving caring or considerate thought, and we may want to be more loving. We may not, however, recognize that part of our loving task is to think about these essential needs for life, liberty, happiness and equality. Life is a constant balancing of these four needs. And being thoughtful about how to best balance them is critical to creating balance in our lives, and to harmonizing.

Creating harmony, and balance, would be a simple matter if meeting life's essentials meant that we were also, automatically, by extension free, equal and happy, but that's not the case. We may take a job which provides the money to meet our life's essentials, but it might underutilize our talents, and so, we may feel unfulfilled and unhappy. We can think of taking a job which we don't want as interfering with our freedom. The point is, we cannot focus on only meeting life's essentials, as if, in satisfying that need, we will meet the others. It takes thought to recognize that our desire for freedom and equality relates to our overall sense of happiness, and to begin to take steps to adjust to create a balance. We can't focus on only one and achieve all four. Without thought, without caring to think about how to balance these ideals in our lives, we fall short of harmonizing.

If we are struggling to resolve the tension between these aims, it can help if we put our cares and thoughts down on paper. Doing so we can follow a train of thought through to a solution. It is actually amazing what the human mind can think through when it focuses on doing so. As Dr. Seuss playfully, but convincingly wrote, "Think left and think right and think low and think high. Oh, the thinks you can think up if only you try!" Consider the thought that went into thinking of that encouraging poetry. And more significantly, consider the thought that went into writing the Constitution, or the Declaration of Independence, or creating a vaccine, or a life-enhancing device like the light bulb, or more recently, the computer. As important as these are, consider the thought that went into the day you moved someone's life. Maybe you went to visit someone at the hospital. Maybe you lent a listening ear and helped a person work through a challenge. Maybe you helped someone discover something meaningful about themselves. Of course, many of these things happen every day, but then there are many days where we might go through life without giving much thought to how to make a difference. By making it a point to think, to be thoughtful, more often, we more often are able to make a difference.

Being thoughtful we are able to create all that we create, we share meaningfully, lift another up, or we brighten another's day.

While thoughtfulness is a powerful tool for harmonizing, we may not use it as much as we can, particularly to solve those challenges that exist in our lives. This is because using thought to resolve challenges takes effort, dedication, commitment and connection to caring.

To make use of thought for our personal challenges and goals, we have to do something akin, in some ways, to figuring out how to align the colors in a Rubik's cube, or akin to playing chess—we have to think about our choices and actions in terms of the various impacts on various people and from various perspectives that those choices and actions will have. While this requires thinking, it's a different type of thinking, in that it involves caring in a way that playing chess or doing a Rubik's cube does not. Yes, they have in common the idea that we have to care in order to solve the challenge. But, in dealing with our personal goal to achieve life, liberty, happiness and equality, there are no clear strategies or directions. And it can be a challenge to be other-focused—to get our thoughts to be focused on others, not only on ourselves (and our "win").

However, like those games, we can study and learn about strategies for breaking through those challenges. That's what reading a book like this, for example, is doing. It's learning to think about creating balance in our lives.

When we think of using thoughtfulness as a tool for creating and constructing, we have to get beyond the notion of thoughtfulness as being about simple things, like remembering a person's birthday, or cleaning up after ourselves, or such conventional notions. Being thoughtful involves thinking more deeply about the meaning of the words *loving, responsive, uniting, equality, happiness, life's essentials, freedom* and so on.

While looking at those words, and concepts, we might give thought to what we are or are not doing well. We might give thought to how to help another. We might give thought to how to use our time better.

Further, being thoughtful means recognizing what it means to be thoughtless, wasting the power we have for thought. We might all know we do a certain amount of this, and kick ourselves for it. But we, actually, may not know how much we do it. To illustrate, with a surprising example, we might ask if watching the news too much, like doing anything too often, is also wasting time. It may seem an odd question. The news may not actually jump out as bad for us, and it may seem surprising for a newspaper to publish an article titled "News is bad for you — and why giving up reading it will make you happier,"[4] but that's exactly what The Guardian did, with Rolf Dobelli's piece. In summary, it says, "News is bad for you. It leads to fear and aggression, and hinders your creativity and ability to think deeply. The solution? Stop consuming it altogether."[5] He notes, "Out of the 10,000 news stories you may have read in the last 12 months, did even one allow you to make a better decision about a serious matter in your life?"[6] He explains that the reason that it has such a negative effect is that you get drawn into the story and it "works like a drug"[7] — you get addicted to every detail, whether important to your life or not. Among his list of reasons that the news is bad for you is that it wastes time. This, of course, could be said of so many other things we spend time doing.

Thoughtfulness is different than mere thinking, in that it involves creating constructive and productive growth. It might require that we take a hobby, or "mindless" activity, and turn it into something more. For example, a person who knits scarfs, or sweaters for friends and family, perhaps, can make them for a non-profit organization that delivers clothes to those who need it. This doesn't take much thought. It may take much more thought to transform other hobbies and activities.

More often, however, we may have to start with a clean slate and give deep thought to a challenge we'd like to become involved with, and then develop the skills to do so.

Transforming our lives to make them more consistently and pervasively thoughtful can happen from taking small, thoughtful steps. Recycling and other actions to prevent global warming, for example, stem from caring thoughts, and may require little steps at a time. With individual heart-felt thought, we reduce our personal carbon footprint. Do you know how to measure your carbon footprint? That's a thoughtful question. To find the answer you can Google search — or, simply go to http://www.nature.org/greenliving/carboncalculator/. In the process, you will be combining your processing capability with your care—or acting thoughtfully. Follow that last step, you can then read about measures you can take to reduce your footprint.

BEING THOUGHTFUL

That's, of course, only one example, but it's a useful example to highlight a point. Thoughtfulness involves identifying what you care about, then thinking about how what you care about affects others, and then adjusting how you give and receive.

Of course, being thoughtful can involve becoming healthier in the physical realm. Counting calories, and watching your weight, through paying attention to a myriad of nutritional factors, for example, is being thoughtful, as our health often affects, not only ourselves, but also others.

It has been said frequently, by many, that we cannot truly care well for others if we do not care for ourselves.[8] The idea is not too much thought about self, not too much about other, but just the right amount about each. And so it takes thought to strike the right balance.

Thought is something the brain can do — we think quite naturally. But thoughtfulness depends upon a loving heart. It's a matter of identifying our care and connecting it to our power to think to create and construct.

Loving thoughts nourish our heart, body and mind and add to the health of humanity. By filling our thoughts with more love we *spread* kindness, peace, harmony and other beautiful energies out into the world, something we all long for.

When we think, or process information to be more caring, we are being thoughtful.

When we think about how we can respond better, we are being thoughtful.

When we think about how we can unite better, we are being thoughtful.

CREATING HARMONY

When we think about how we can individualize better, we are being thoughtful.

When we think about how we can be more sensitive, we are being thoughtful.

When we think about how we can be more meaningful, we are being thoughtful.

When we think about how we can be more empathetic, we are being thoughtful.

8

Being Responsive

"Until the great mass of the people shall be filled with the sense of responsibility for each other's welfare, social justice can never be attained."

- Helen Keller

CREATING HARMONY

Body part: nerves (for protecting and comforting)

Nerves are to the Body

as Responsiveness is to Harmonious Action,

in that both, nerves and responsiveness, involve responding to keep us safe, happy and free of unnecessary pain.

The nerves, in the healthy body, automatically respond to stimuli that bring the body pleasure or pain. We, in our lives, also respond to things that bring us pleasure or pain. We tend to be drawn to those things that bring us pleasure and to avoid those things that bring us pain — although, we do this imperfectly. As our nerves respond automatically in our body to messages that keep our body safe, happy, and healthy, so, too, in our lives, we can respond to one another in courageous ways that increase the safety, happiness and harmony of our relationships.

Responsive is defined as "reacting quickly and positively."[9] The healthy nerves do this naturally. To do this in our lives requires effort and intention. It does not come naturally in many situations. And so we have to learn how to do it.

We can begin by recognizing that we have a need for the general categories, which we've explained are in tension: those, again, to life, liberty, happiness and equality. By recognizing that we have these needs, we can begin to better respond to them.

Valuing equality, we respond in ways that value others as much as ourselves. We begin to recognize when we are not respecting or regarding others' needs and when others are not respecting or regarding our own needs. And by recognizing this, we are better able to guide our responses.

BEING RESPONSIVE

Valuing life's essentials, we respond in ways that appreciate, rather than take for granted, the essentials of life. We regard having food, water and shelter as being meaningful, and concern ourselves with whether others have these as well. Stopping for a moment and being grateful for something very basic that we have can help us to respond better than we would if, instead, we were to focus on what we want, but don't need.

Valuing happiness, we respond in ways that lead to both short and long-term happiness. The nerves actually respond to both short and long-term happiness — we might want the pizza the minute it comes out of the oven, but from past experience, we know to wait. Or, our hand draws back from something hot that we might want, as we reach for it. Similarly, in our lives, we know to wait on some things—"good things come to those who wait," so the expression goes.

And valuing happiness, we respond in ways that increase *others'* short and long-term happiness. We may give up that extra hour of television, or we may give up that Saturday of golf, to use the time more considerately.

It's not only the choice of our activities, which makes us responsive or not, it's also how we respond in our activities, of course. Consider a simple example, we may "bite our tongue" to keep from saying something brash or hurtful. Responsive to another's happiness, we check ourselves in innumerous ways. If we keep, more ever-present in our minds, a goal for those around us to be happy, we can be even more responsive to them. We shout less, we snap less, we may ignore less, we do less of what others dislike and more of what other's rightly want and need. Considering the impacts on others' happiness can help us balance our counter tendency to focus on the short-term and too much on ourselves.

CREATING HARMONY

Valuing freedom, we respond in ways that respect our own and others' needs for space and time. When we think of freedom, we can think of space and time. To make the point in a stark way, think of a prison sentence where freedom is taken—the term is measured in time and space. Of course, it's also measured in what one is allowed or not allowed to do. The point is, when we value freedom, we can respond in ways which promote free expression in our activities.

Being responsive, acting like a nerve, takes the courage, or nerve, to regulate ourselves, and our desires. We might want to take a job which pays a lot, even though it may strain our family, because we're afraid we can't survive without it or we want the extra "goodies" (the boat, the more expensive car, or bigger house) it brings. A more courageous and responsible choice might be to take a lower paying job, which is more meaningful, and which leaves us time to be more nurturing in our relationships. When either fear, or excessive desire, wanting more than we actually need, is the main driver for a choice, we often wind up feeling unfulfilled. As Plato said, "Courage is knowing what not to fear." When we stop responding to the desire for short-term pleasure from leisure and entertainment, and, instead, start responding to the desire for deeper pleasure from making deeper connections with ourselves and others, these new responses create healthy changes in our relationships and lives.

If we feel overwhelmed or entrenched in our current lifestyle, struggling to break free of a rat race, we can develop the ability to more courageously respond by starting small and simplifying. By simplifying our lives, we can find time for the activities we know are more meaningful. Shutting off the TV, we make space for thought, and we make more space to be more responsive to the challenges we face.

Identifying a place where we can be healthier is a good first step. Then, committing to take a small step towards making a change is a strong next step. We may give up smoking or drinking to make room for healthier habits. We may give up overindulgences in sports or shopping to make room for more meaningful pursuits. We may let go of an unhealthy relationship to make room for a more loving relationship. As the famous saying by Alexander Graham Bell goes, "when one door closes another opens." The saying continues, "but we often look so long and so regretfully upon the closed door that we do not see the one which has opened for us." As we let go of the closed doors, our responses change.

Learning about our responses involves learning to recognize how, when, who and what to respond to. So many of our responses are triggered by the carrot and stick, the reward we're seeking or the penalty we fear. If we can identify the rewards that we can get from a particular step, or the penalties that might come from a particular activity, we can begin to change the way we respond. A common example of a reward, which might motivate, is being able to fit into the outfit we want to fit into, motivating us to diet. Or, we might be motivated by the fear of being seen critically at an event. These are external motivators. We can also be motivated by intrinsic motivators. An intrinsic motivation for dieting would be because we value and enjoying eating healthy—for its own sake. The intrinsic reward is felt as we're eating healthy foods, much as the intrinsic penalty is felt as we're eating poorly. The carrot and stick, whether external or internal, can be powerful motivators if we consciously pay attention to them.

CREATING HARMONY

Ultimately, we do not want to be motivated by the external carrot or stick, we want to be motivated to do those things for the sake of the activity, the intrinsic value of the activity—that is, the joy we want to strive for is the joy that comes with the doing, not with the getting or not getting. When we rake the leaves, or do the dishes, we want to do it because of the joy we get in doing it, not solely because of the goal of getting the task done. Certainly, there must be purpose in the doing, but there must be joy in the doing as well. We can say this about the mundane tasks or the noble and ambitious ones. When Gandhi sought freedom for India, for example, he derived joy from working toward that goal and achieving the goal. When King sought freedom and equality for blacks, he, too, derived a sense of satisfaction from both the working toward the goal and the achievements along the way. Further, in our everyday lives, when we love our work and our work makes a difference, when we love our families and relationships and they make a difference, because we are responding to deeper needs, we feel fulfilled from the process of doing, or giving, not just from the getting.

We find this joy and satisfaction as we learn to balance our own needs with those of others. Responding only, or predominately, to our own and not also to others' desires and fears, invariably, results in disappointment and dissatisfaction. Responding in balance, we increase beauty in the world because balance is the ideal nature of things — and it leads to what we might call "satisfied customers."

From the ancient Greeks to today, there is considerable belief in the idea of the mean, which is the middle between the extremes, and this is what we want to guide our responses to achieve. Aristotle's golden mean is the middle state. In Christianity, Aquinas asserted "moral virtue observes the mean."[10] In Islam, Mohammad had a saying translated as "the best choice is the middle ground/golden mean one."[11] And Buddha's path is the Middle Way, a path between "religious asceticism and worldly self-indulgence."[12] So, we want to be responsive to the need for balance.

While this idea of the middle between the extremes reflects the idea of balance, the question in our responses is what to balance. We've been suggesting the goal is to balance the tension between the need for life, liberty, happiness and equality, our own need for these, and others' need for these.

As we guide our responses to bringing these about, we experience greater balance and a sense of harmony with others. It only makes sense that as we care, think and respond to our own and others most sacred needs, we foster harmony.

9

Being Uniting

"A human being is part of a whole, called by us the Universe, a part limited in time and space. He experiences himself, his thoughts and feelings, as something separated from the rest a kind of optical delusion of his consciousness. This delusion is a kind of prison for us, restricting us to our personal desires and to affection for a few persons nearest us. Our task must be to free ourselves from this prison by widening our circles of compassion to embrace all living creatures and the whole of nature in its beauty."

- Albert Einstein

BEING UNITING

Body part: Tendons (for flexibly connecting)

Tendons are to the Body
as Being Uniting is to Harmonious Action,
in that both, the tendons and being uniting, involve connecting.

Many of us may regard being uniting, and connecting with others, as being important, even necessary, to our ability to succeed and live fulfilling lives. Of course, uniting is a large part of most of our lives. Many of us work in companies or organizations which depend upon other co-workers. And those of us who don't, nonetheless, depend upon others in innumerous ways, including for the goods and services we receive and for the activities we engage in—"no man is an island," so the expression goes. And yet, we may not think we can learn much more about the concept than we already know.

Yet, we can improve in our ability to unite by recognizing uniting with others as being similar to the value the tendons play in uniting bones with muscles. In so doing, the tendons provide strength and flexibility. Similarly, when we strive to unite with others we achieve more strength and flexibility.

And the role of strength and flexibility is clear: with strength and flexibility physical structures are able to withstand tension. Similarly, with flexibility in our relationships tensions and stresses can be overcome.

With flexibility we consider another's point of view. We open to new activities. We break patterns or habits that are counterproductive and form ones that are constructive and productive. We give and receive better.

We can think of the give and take of uniting as sometimes sharing and sometimes receiving, sometimes holding firm and sometimes letting go, sometimes leading and sometimes being led. Good teamwork is uniting, and is built upon give and take, as many of us know. One person plays shortstop, another catcher.... One person is strong in marketing, another at finance. One person is a good writer, another a good editor, etc.

When people come together bringing their individual talents well together, the sum is greater than the parts. As many point out, the union of two individuals brings about a third unit, the relationship, or what some might call the unity, or union of the two. The two become one, a much stronger whole unit.

The unity exhibited in sports, corporations and organizations exhibits this. And we might point out that it leads to connections between people that might not otherwise happen. In sports, we see racial divides come down. In business, we see people working together from distant countries despite different religions and ideologies. With non-profits, we see people coming together to unite the resources of those who have with those who do not. All these developments are accomplished because of the give and take of uniting.

And countries, of course, reflect unities which provide strength and flexibility, with give and take. The United States reflects the union of states, and the United Nations reflects the union of the world's countries. The choice of the word *united* in those names reflects the recognition that there is strength in union —united we stand, divided we fall.

In uniting, we can find common principles to unite differing points of view. Through the sharing and give and take, the flexibility and the integrating of two, or many, into one, with the realization that we're not so different, peace is often forged, where otherwise there would be war. When we unite and connect with others, we move beyond treating differences as reasons for separation and anger. Our interest in combining strengths, by being flexible, allows us to see opport*unities* to come together for mutual solutions.

Of course, it is important to recognize that not all unities are good: the purpose of a particular union must be constructive and harmonizing for it to be considered good. Again, as with thoughtfulness and responsiveness, when uniting is guided for the purpose of bringing about life, liberty, happiness and equality, in balance, and for all, it is a uniting for harmony. Uniting with others, near and far, for freedom, happiness, life's essentials, and equality for all, we create more peace and prosperity.

10

Being Individualizing

"To be yourself in a world that is constantly trying to make you something else is the greatest accomplishment."

- Ralph Waldo Emerson

BEING INDIVIDUALIZING

Body part: Bones (for supporting)

Bones are to the Body

as Individualizing is to Harmonious Action,

in that both, the bones and being individualizing, involve supporting, and providing structure for the whole.

Acting with individuality, we bring our unique gifts to others and, thereby, provide a support structure for our relationships. Much as our bones give our body its unique individual support structure, expressing our individuality, or fulfilling our unique purpose, gives our lives and relationships a support structure.

When we think of the great examples of individuality, we may have a tendency to think of the Olympian, inventor, successful entrepreneur, world traveler, or those who take the less worn path in one way or another. But beyond that, expressing individuality means being uniquely contributory in even everyday ways. It's in expressing ourselves with integrity in our everyday relationships and interactions.[13]

It's not always easy to express individuality in ways which are constructive and contributing. In our society today, individuality is encouraged in some ways but discouraged in others. Often it is encouraged in the dress code or in outer appearances, and where stardom is valued, in sports and entertainment, but it is discouraged in the workplace. At work, people are encouraged to take and follow directions, and often, discouraged from sharing ideas or making changes. Though companies may have suggestion boxes, seeking input and ideas from employees, it takes a whole lot more for a unique idea to be nurtured from idea to fruition, and many employees are rarely made part of that process.

The key to bringing out the positive value of individuality is to encourage people to share their unique gifts for the good of others. And not only encourage it, but also facilitate and nurture it. Individualizing people are people who recognize the value of their own worth, and develop their unique gifts for the purpose of serving others. Such individuals need an environment which receives and embraces them for those efforts in order to help their efforts to blossom.

It is a sharing process. It is an interdependent process. One cannot share without another who is willing to embracingly receive their gifts.[14] One cannot give without someone to give to.

We can encourage individuality better by first recognizing that it provides a strong foundation, like the bones, from which to build upon. All structures are unique, and it is from that uniqueness, or variation, that both the individual and the group are able to grow and flourish. The idea of building a better mousetrap is a conventional one in the business world, and is known for being necessary for business growth. The idea of evolution is that new species and survival capabilities are spawned by individuality. Even a species such as humans are dependent upon the unique gifts of species, such as bees for pollination. As one science writer puts it, succinctly, "without bees, humans would starve."[15] It is the diversity, which is an element of individuality, that is at the foundation of interdependence. By promoting the idea that individuals contribute best when they identify their unique gifts and identify how they can share them, we increase our chances of success as a unit.

BEING INDIVIDUALIZING

Yet, despite the great importance of individuality, how often do people recognize that they have a unique gift to share? This is, in part, because individuals thwart their own ability to discover their unique gifts, thinking that they are not free to discover them. They may follow the discouraging words of others, or what they're told they should do even if they themselves have a better way. It's also, in part, because people tend to spend more time looking to consume than looking for new and novel ways to produce, or contribute.

Advertisements abound, and guide people: people often follow what others tell them that they ought to value. They follow, not an inner guide, or inner spirit, or higher power, which tells them that they are free and equally worthy to think and feel as they do, and to contribute in ways they believe are valuable and important, but instead, the advertisements which tell them how they ought to look, what they ought to be interested in, and how they should spend their time. Media, of course, shapes people's perceptions as to what is valuable and what is worthy. More often people are told that this or that product is the one that they need rather than being told that what they need is to be the one to create their own worth and service.

So, when looking for a unique gift, or purpose, it is best to start by asking yourself how you feel you can contribute. And then start taking steps to make that contribution.

Developing your gift means accepting the fact that others around you may not be interested in what you have to offer, but that there are others who will be. As one literary agent advises authors, don't worry if not everyone loves what you write, there are likely others who will find what you write valuable. The same is true in all walks of life and with all unique gifts.

CREATING HARMONY

In developing our gifts, we can strengthen our ability to connect by looking for ways to express individuality with integrity. The offering of individuality is best when it has the integrity to create a strong support structure for our relations. A beautiful example of this type of individuality is of Rosa Parks standing up against racism by staying seated at the front of a bus, in 1955, when blacks were expected to give up their seat at the front of the bus for whites. She stayed seated, standing up, not for those who thought blacks should be subjugated to whites, but instead for the principle of equal worth. Though, initially, she was punished for it, in the end she and equality prevailed. Acting with a belief in her individual worth, she changed the structure of the system. Isn't that individuality with integrity?[16]

Of course, there are many everyday examples of individuality. When we stand up to an unethical boss, that's individuality. When, as a young child, we walk away from a group of misbehaving peers and do the right thing, that's individuality. When we move away from gossip, or hurtful conversation, that's individuality. Individuality is doing the right thing in our relationships and jobs. It's in the integrity we bring to our everyday moments.[17]

Great individuals are ordinary people who act with integrity, when expressing their individuality. They extend themselves, in part, to express their unique strengths and gifts and, in part, to stand up for others who need them. In each of us is a great individual. Like the bones, we stand up straight when we stand up for ourselves in all our beauty, and when we assert our true purpose for the good of all.

Of course, individuality must connect with each of the other behaviors for it to be expressed in ways that contribute.

BEING INDIVIDUALIZING

Individuality with love.
When we develop and express our unique talents in ways that are attentive to the needs of others, we are expressing our individuality with love.

Individuality with thoughtfulness.
When we think about how to develop and express our unique talents we are being individualizing with thoughtfulness.

Individuality with responsiveness.
When we respond uniquely to others in ways that bring about life's essentials, happiness, freedom and equality, we are being individualizing with responsiveness.

Individuality with uniting.
When we unite with others, embracing their strengths and lending our own, we are being individualizing while uniting.

Individuality with sensitivity.
When we sense how another is feeling with our own unique perception, we are being individualizing with sensitivity.

Individuality with meaningfulness.
When we dare to be different, to make a difference in another's life, we are being individualizing in a meaningful way.

Individuality with empathy.
When, in our own unique way, we put ourselves in another shoes, we are being individualizing and empathetic.

11

Being Sensitive

"The sensitivity of men to small matters, and their indifference to great ones, indicates a strange inversion."

- Blaise Pascal

BEING SENSITIVE

Body part: Senses (for sensing)

Senses are to the Body

as Sensitivity is to Harmonious Action,

in that both, senses and being sensitive, involve sensing and detecting.

In our relationships, our sensitivity allows us to feel how we are feeling and to see and feel how another is feeling. We may notice a smile or a frown on another, and because our senses work with our brain, we are able to discern the meaning of what we see.

Our feelings help us to experience the fullness of the world in obvious ways. We feel good by an embracing touch. We feel moved when we see a magnificent sunset. We feel excited when we smell our favorite dish being cooked. We feel a sense of wonder and connection to our earth during a walk along the beach as we take in the smell of the ocean air. All these things we sense; all these things we feel. It is our ability to sense that allows us to feel (see, hear, taste, touch) the beauty of the world around us.[18]

Similarly, beyond physically sensing, it is our ability to behave sensitively that extends the power of physical sense into our interpersonal relationships. By being sensitive, we are able to create positive and constructive experiences and interactions.

If we are not generally in touch with our feelings or with others' feelings, we might try using our senses to become sensitive. Many of us want people to be more sensitive to our feelings. Likely, we, too, can be more sensitive to others' feelings by seeing, hearing, watching body language, and listening for content and tone. How often have we said something which we should have known another would not feel good hearing, but we did so because we weren't thinking about their feelings? Being sensitive involves using thought, much as thoughtfulness involves using care. The heart, senses, and brain connect for physical sense, so too, caring, or being loving, and being thoughtful combine with sensitivity.

Of course, there are cultural forces that make being sensitive in day-to-day life, a challenge. We lose the personal touch when we have a meeting over the phone rather than in person. We may engage in life more vicariously, spending more time watching television and videos than we do creating or interacting with others.

Not only does technology distance us from others in those ways, it also distances us when it desensitizes us. The graphic nature of what's shown in many video games, some music videos, and on many television shows, or YouTube videos can desensitize us to harmful behaviors. It may make us more inclined to use language which is degrading or insensitive.

And yet, there is much that is good about technology. It can bring the world closer to us. It can inform us of the challenges that others in a world far away face. And the ease and rapidity with which we can communicate over distances, both far and near, can help us to be more responsive and more sensitive. We can more easily communicate more information, which can help us to be more nuanced, and thereby, more uniting and sensitive, if we use it to do so.

The trick is to use technology in ways that help us to be more sensitive. Many communications are difficult to have by text or email, or even by phone. Sensitive topics, ones where someone's feelings might be hurt by what has to be discussed, benefit, often, by having a conversation in person where the observation of body language can provide insight into feelings, and where we can use a comforting touch, and even the power of a first-hand smile to be comforting.

With our senses and a window into our own and others' feelings, we connect with the world around us and to what others need, and, in so doing, we are better able to connect and lift each other up.

To get better at becoming sensitive, the next time you are in a conversation with someone, use your senses to sense how they are feeling — don't just listen to what they are saying, engage your eyes and your brain. And, importantly, use your heart, not just metaphorically. Your heart pumps blood to your brain. So, too, the heart pumps energy between two people, so recognize that you want to put your heart into listening too. Allow yourself to deeply understand what they are saying on a feeling level. Do you feel good? Do they feel good?

And when someone is feeling badly, maybe a gentle touch or a pat on the back is what they need. Or, perhaps a silent, open, listening ear is just the right "touch." With a desire to balance our own feelings and needs with those of others, we can make use of our senses to inform us of what we need to know to act in balance with others, all others.[19]

Companies actually utilize the sensing function, as well, when they solicit and listen to customer feedback, as only one example. When they measure their performance according to various factors, such as sales and profits, too, they are using the sensing function.

Whether at work or in our personal lives, in our relationships with each other, we can share the grace and beauty of our feelings. As we allow our caring, sensitive feelings to flow through us and into the lives of others, we heal each other. Through the gift of sensitivity, as we open our eyes and ears to what is being shared, and what is being needed, we strengthen our bonds. By becoming more gentle and caring, we become more strongly connected to one another.

Perhaps, today, more than ever, there is a great call for sensitivity to reclaim the wonder and power it has to connect us in meaningful and healing ways. The grace and beauty of aligned sensitivity in our acts will undoubtedly lead us toward better connections, more love, more joy and fulfillment for all.

And to be sure, sensitivity does not require "vision" or other senses — it can be enhanced by it, but as Helen Keller well proved, with her sensitive insights, we can overcome the limits of the senses. As she said, "the only thing worse than being blind is having sight but no vision." Using our senses to get in touch with our feelings and others' feelings we have inner vision.

12

Being Meaningful

"Many persons have a wrong idea of what constitutes true happiness. It is not attained through self-gratification but through fidelity to a worthy purpose."

- Helen Keller

CREATING HARMONY

Body part: Muscles (for moving)

Muscles are to the Body
as Meaningfulness is to Harmonious Action,
in that both, muscles and meaningfulness, involve moving.

We may not give much thought to the idea of meaningfulness, and yet, likely, all of us want our lives to be meaningful.

To think about meaningfulness, we can begin by thinking about the meaning of meaning. Most of us, likely, regard being understanding as an important quality for achieving harmony. But we may not recognize the importance of developing meaning as a prerequisite to being understanding.

Naturally, meaning would be essential to creating harmony. Without meaning we cannot understand one another; it is meaning that allows for shared understanding. We give the word *water* to a liquid and with that meaning we can coordinate and communicate to get it, give it, or share it.

As we venture into giving and receiving, and sharing those things which are not tangible, meaning becomes even more important and more difficult to exchange. Beyond basic items, such as food and water, which have obvious essential meaning and value, there are the myriad of things we exchange and share which may or may not have obvious significance or value. And so, we are in a constant state of evaluating the meaningfulness of things to determine how valuable something is.

BEING MEANINGFUL

Since meaningful things are those which are "significant, relevant, important, consequential, telling, material, valid, worthwhile"[20] it's up to us to discern what has this value. It's up to us to give significance to our day-to-day interactions by getting better at sharing with value.

The reason that meaningfulness is so closely related to significance can be simply explained. Imagine speaking Swahili to someone who only speaks English. Without meaning being exchanged it's not a very fruitful conversation. We don't want our lives to be full of that type of exchange. All of what we do is simply an extension of, or form of, language exchange. The products and services we make and exchange are material forms of significance and value (value of varying degrees). A cup, for example, holds liquid and thus has value.

So, in an effort to make things that have more meaning, we can learn how meaning is developed and fostered. Taking a simple example, we develop our ability to convey meaningfully with language by practicing our ability to do so, by expanding our vocabulary and, through trial and error, speaking with others, and seeing how well or not so well we communicate. Much as, with writing, it takes practice, writing and re-writing, so too, with developing our ability to provide meaningful products and services, or meaning in our relationships, it takes practice, and it takes constantly striving to improve the value of what we have to share.

This effort at improving, or developing, our ability to share meaningfully is similar to the way we develop muscles in the body. Our muscles grow by stretching and repetition against resistance and force. So, too, we develop how, and what, we are able to contribute, or our meaningfulness, by stretching and repetition against resistance and force, distractions, uncertainties, fears, etc.

To connect with this idea of developing meaningfulness in our lives, we might think of how we've developed a talent or a skill to a point where we now feel we can provide something of value. And we also may think about what others have done that we found meaningful and how hard they worked to provide it. We might think of a favorite teacher who made a meaningful difference in our life, or of a moving book, or artwork, or of advice someone's given us that changed our life, and take a moment to think about all that went into their being able to do so.

It is fairly easy to see that developing our ability to contribute meaningfully takes effort. It may be harder to figure out what would be a meaningful career for us to develop, and even harder to find what we might call a meaningful job. But, here, too, we can liken our ability to develop a meaningful career or job to how we come to understand anything: by delving into its meaning. That is, we can start to evaluate what it is that makes work meaningful for us. Is it working with people, face to face? Is it working by ourselves? Is it helping others with a service, or is it in making a product? These kinds of questions help us to better understand what makes something meaningful to us.

Of course, so many of us don't know what we find meaningful, in part, because our desires for short-term pleasure interfere with our thinking about it. And also, in part, because our fears may keep us from responding to the challenges that arise in developing a meaningful job or career. This is compounded by the fact that society doesn't encourage people to think about or pursue meaningfulness so much as it encourages people to do things that "make a living." And often, it even encourages people to engage in excessive entertainment, addictive indulgences and amoral living.[21]

Though these cultural forces might be working against those who want to discover what they find meaningful, each of us can begin by considering what we love to do. And from there, we can begin to discover where we might be of the greatest service. We may enjoy playing an instrument, coaching, gardening, community service, or building and fixing things. Practicing those areas where we feel drawn to make a difference, we get better and we begin to increase our ability to share meaningfully.

We can stretch ourselves with our families and friends to cultivate strong bonds based on active living, rather than ones which are based on vicarious living, watching television, bands, and sports. We can devote more time to fostering care, and deepening understanding, and give less time to acquiring and accumulating. We can form friendships that work to address a cause rather than ones which involve competing for a medal or a trophy. Meaningful living does not come from without, it doesn't come from winning the lottery, or good "fortune," so much as it comes from finding what moves our own and others' hearts, minds and bodies. As Maya Angelou notes of writing, "The idea is to write it so that people hear it and it slides through the brain and goes straight to the heart." She could add, "and so that they are moved to act lovingly and harmoniously." This applies to any activity.

So, on your journey to develop meaning in your life, find something that moves your heart, something that you like to do that adds value to others too, and reach for it. If it is purposeful, and relates to bringing about more life's essentials, happiness, equality and liberty for others, then learn to make it so that it moves others in body, mind and heart.

CREATING HARMONY

Meaningfulness with love.

When we move products, services and information to become more caring, by putting our time, attention, and affection to doing so, we are acting meaningfully with love.

Meaningfulness with thoughtfulness.

When we move products, services and information to become more thoughtful, we are being meaningful and thoughtful.

Meaningfulness with responsiveness.

When we move products, services and information to respond in ways that respect our own and others' life's essentials, need for liberty, equality, and happiness, we are acting meaningfully and responsively.

Meaningfulness with uniting.

When we move products, services and information to become more connecting with others in ways that value others' contribution and strengths, we are acting meaningfully and unitingly.

Meaningfulness with individuality.

When we move products, services and information to bring our unique strengths to light we are acting meaningfully with individuality.

Meaningfulness with sensitivity.

When we move products, services and information to better detect and honor the value of feelings, we are acting meaningfully and sensitively.

BEING MEANINGFUL

Meaningfulness with empathy.

When we move products, services and information to improve others' lives, for constructive growth and health, we are acting meaningfully and empathetically.

13

Being Empathetic

"There are many respects in which America, if it can bring itself to act with the magnanimity and the empathy appropriate to its size and power, can be an intelligent example to the world."

- J. William Fulbright

BEING EMPATHETIC

Body part: Limbic system (for energizing)

The Limbic System (for emotions) is to the Body
as Empathy is to Harmonious Action,
in that both, the limbic system (for emotions) and empathy,
energize.

Empathy, some say, is the essential component for human connection, in that it is what allows us to feel for another and to act in ways that lift another up. But unlike that conventional notion, which views empathy as the critical link, we say it is one vital part among many, and it is vital, in that it provides the *energy* for harmonious connection.

Much as the limbic system, the seat of the emotions, is energizing, so too, empathy is energizing. It is what allows us to care for others and to energize others with that care. It is what connects our emotions of love and concern to the emotions of another.

Neuroscientists suggest the basis of our ability for empathy is what are called mirror neurons. When we look at another and see what they are feeling, we are able to understand and even experience the feeling because of the connection between the mirror neurons and the limbic system.[22] In other words, when we feel empathy for another, our neurons, which detect the experience of another, are connecting with our emotional center, and, in so doing, allowing us to show care and concern. Thus, we are transforming a "negative" energy into a more "positive" energy.

CREATING HARMONY

Empathy, of course, is a behavior, and energizing is a function. So, the analogy we are making here, between empathy, the behavior, and the limbic system, or emotions, is that both are energizing. What this means is that we may want to bring into our interactions and relationships more empathy, in order to energize and transform negative energies. How often do we resist the challenges that another faces and wants to share? Empathy is putting our power to experience emotions to work in a positive way.

Empathy has the power to lift others up, and ourselves up too. Acting with empathy, we use our emotions for love, understanding and compassion, and, in so doing, not only help others to feel better, but help ourselves to feel better, as we see in "our mirror," a sense of relief, or improvement.

And so, empathy energizes like all positive emotions do, but because it helps transform a feeling of sorrow, it is even more powerful.

We can develop our ability to be more empathetic. We can learn to look for ways to put ourselves in another's shoes. Look across the room, see someone and imagine that you are them. Imagine looking like them, thinking like them, speaking like them, dealing with what they are dealing with. Do this on a regular basis. As you do it more and more you will develop a better sense of self in relation to others. And you will likely develop a sense of appreciation and deeper gratitude for what you have — for your talents and blessings. And beyond how it will change your perception of others and of your own life, many people suggest that empathizing with others will also make others more inclined to empathize with you too.

To better understand what empathy is, we can think of being embracing and encouraging as two complementary, or supporting, traits. Embracing, we accept and receive another. Encouraging, we give courage to others when times are bad, when things are difficult. Naturally, support groups provide empathy for people who share a similar challenge by being embracing and also by providing encouragement.

Empathy reveals itself not only through support of someone who is suffering but also in actions that help prevent future suffering. For example, someone may lose someone to a drunk driver and then work to bring greater awareness about the problem in order to help prevent it from happening to another. Or someone may experience a cancer and then work to raise money for better treatment and a cure. The experience of a loss can help us to relate to and care about the risks to others. If you are looking for ways to find meaning and purpose, one place to begin is by thinking of challenges that people face and looking for ways to empathize, ways to lift others up.

How often do we reach out beyond our closest circles to empathize with someone far away, or in a dramatically different circumstance than us? If we want to increase our ability to energize others, we have to increase our ability to empathize. As Jeremy Rifkin, an economic and social theorist, in *The Empathic Civilization* notes, over time, humans have broadened their empathy beyond the tribe, to the nation, and, more recently, and more significantly, to the world. He and others suggest that this power for broadening our ability to empathize is critical to our ability, as a species, to deal with global challenges and to achieve world peace.

When we begin to empathize with the need for all peoples to have their life's essentials, to pursue happiness, in freedom and equality, we can guide our behaviors to help fulfill these needs throughout the world.

CREATING HARMONY

When we energize others by giving our time, attention, affection and resources to seeing the world through their eyes, we are empathizing with love.

When we give thought to better understanding how another feels, and share in the feeling of the other, we are being empathetic and thoughtful.

When we respond to how another feels, and share in the feeling of the other, we are being empathetic and responsive.

When we connect with others' challenges and feelings, and share in the feelings of the others, we are being empathetic and uniting.

When we express our unique gifts to help another feel understood, and share in the feeling of the other, we are being empathetic and individualizing.

When we are sensitive to the feelings of another, and share in the feeling of that other, we are being empathetic and sensitive.

When we share in the feeling of another, and we make a difference in another's life, moving them to feel better and grow, after they've faced a challenge, we are being empathetic and meaningful.

Extending our hearts outward to feel how another feels we blossom in our acts of compassion. We heal through empathy and compassion as we learn and understand, in our heart, that another, whether near or far, familiar or unfamiliar, has the same longings and needs that we have. We all long for peace, safety, freedom, and joy. Without them we suffer. With them, we link with one another and blossom as though we were one.[23]

KEY VALUES

Function	Body	Value
Catalyzing	Enzyme	Happiness
Distributing	Circulation	Equality
Venting/ Voicing	Lungs	Freedom
Assimilating	Cell	Life's essentials

14

Being Happy

"Love is that condition in which the happiness of another person is essential to your own."

- Robert A. Heinlein

BEING HAPPY

Body part: Enzymes (for catalyzing)

Enzymes are to the Body

as Happiness is to Harmonious Action,

in that both, enzymes and happiness, involve catalyzing constructive reactions.

Most of us would probably say that happiness must be part of a harmonious relationship, and though we may not think it is an element of all harmonious interactions, when we look at what happiness is, when we define it in a particular way, we see that it is essential to all harmonious relationships.

Happiness is, according to many great thinkers, the experience which results from cultivating values, or engaging in moral actions. As George Washington said, "Happiness and moral duty are inseparably connected."

But what makes up a moral action? And can we distinguish between happiness and moral action? Gandhi said, "Happiness is when what you think, what you say, and what you do are in harmony." We further offer that creating harmonious alignment between what you think, say, and do is about bringing together several facets, or behaviors, for harmony. Happiness becomes a part of alignment; it becomes a component of harmony; it becomes a value that guides us, along with other values, such as life, and life's essentials, liberty, and equality.

If we think of happiness in conventional terms, we might recognize it as satisfaction, "I am happy with my meal." Or, we might recognize it as willingness, "I am happy to do that." Or, we might recognize it as pleasure, "She looked happy."[24]

95

CREATING HARMONY

If we try to foster this type of happiness, and those feelings, what we are doing is acting like an enzyme, and catalyzing positive reactions. The enzyme is described as a lock and key, whereby, a fit is being created.[25] We can work to create a similar type fit when we attempt to create happiness. "Enzymes are usually very specific as to which reactions they catalyze and the substrates that are involved in these reactions. Complementary shape, charge and hydrophilic/hydrophobic characteristics of enzymes and substrates are responsible for this specificity."[26] What the comparison to an enzyme suggests is that we want to tailor our efforts to achieve happiness in a way that creates constructive fits. Tell a joke at the wrong time, to the wrong person, or in the wrong way and the joke does not bring about happiness. So too, engage in an activity at the wrong time or in the wrong way—or engage in the wrong activity, for that matter —and the activity doesn't bring about happiness.

There is nothing particularly surprising about these descriptions of how happiness is fostered.

But what we may not think about is how much fostering happiness, in our own lives, and in the lives of others, is about making what we do fit like a lock and key.

That is, we may do a lot on autopilot, not giving much thought to how much happiness we are fostering. Do we watch movies out of habit? How much enjoyment do we get from them? Do we watch television because there is nothing else to do? If so, then we may benefit by exploring other possibilities.

And how well do we measure our own happiness? Do we take note when we are not happy? And when we are? And importantly, do we pay as much attention to others' happiness and how we factor into their happiness? Do we respond to what they need? Each of these questions is identifying the lock and key, the lock and key being very specific ways in which we are or are not happy. If we want to improve in the area of happiness, we can think of specific areas where we can improve. Are there habits we can change? Are there ways of speaking or interacting we can change? Enzymes create over 4000 different constructive reactions. We can work on our ability to increase our repertoire for creating happiness.

And we might want to create our own happiness index. We can select a handful of categories to measure our happiness. Are we happy with our friends? Our spouse or partner? Our children? Our parents? Our extended family? Our co-workers?

The United Nations has a happiness index it uses to assess how happy people are in different countries. They use the following criteria: "GDP per head, 'healthy life expectancy,' 'having someone to count on,' 'perceived freedom to make life choices,' freedom from corruption, and prevalence of generosity."[27]

Consider the idea of a Gross National Happiness, which is different than a Gross National Product, utilized by Bhutan, which considers the following categories:

1. Psychological wellbeing

2. Health

3. Time use

4. Education

5. Cultural diversity and resilience

6. Good Governance

7. Community vitality

8. Ecological diversity and resilience

CREATING HARMONY

9. Living standard[28]

Once we recognize the areas where we are not catalyzing happiness in our own life, or in other's lives, we can work to improve.

What we want to do is think of our happiness in terms of how often we are smiling and laughing while also demonstrating other moral behaviors and working toward living with values. If we are smiling and laughing often, through simple pleasures, and exhibiting these behaviors of alignment, and realizing these values, we will be happier in the short and long-term.

15

Being Equal

"Whatever is my right as a man is also the right of another; and it becomes my duty to guarantee as well as to possess."

- Thomas Paine

CREATING HARMONY

Body part: Veins (for distributing)

Veins are to the Body

as Equality is to Harmonious Action,

in that both, the veins and equality, involve distributing resources widely.

We can make great strides in our ability to harmonize with others by recognizing that treating others as equals brings about harmony. When we distribute resources in such a way as to balance our own needs with those of others, we sow seeds that come back in reciprocal ways. Creating equality is distributing, not only material resources, of course, but also, intangibles, such as respect, which can be shown in the way we give our attention and affection. When we show equal respect for others, in the way we talk to others and listen to others, it fosters good feelings and warm regards. And it feels good to give in such a way.

Often, we may not think about whether we feel we are being treated equally or treating others equally. Of course, we may think about it when we feel that we are being treated unfairly in some way. If, for example, we are not given what someone else is given, we may think about it and question why.

There is a sense in all of us that there ought to be a fair playing field where we each have the same chance to achieve and receive the fruits of our work.

And, yet, though we are all created equal, the world is not created equally. There are differences in the resources available throughout the world. The climate in some areas is too hot or too cold for agriculture, the availability of oil, important for innumerous essential needs, ranges from non-existent to abundant in different places. And clean water, itself, ranges from available to unavailable or inaccessible. These are only a few examples of how the world, the natural resources of the world, are not equally available to the world's population. Of course, if people could migrate from place to place, freely, and have the access and resources to meet their needs, then society might leave it to individuals to fend for themselves. But in a world cordoned off by country borders and political systems, and with financial resources allocated by legal rules, it becomes incumbent on the haves to consider the needs of the have-nots.

The idea that we have some responsibility for others is, perhaps, what separates us from animals. And we, being at the top of the food chain, might think of this as, "with rights come responsibilities." In the words of the Universal Declaration of Human Rights "the foundation of freedom, justice and peace" is the "recognition of the inherent dignity and of the equal and inalienable rights of all members of the human family."[29] In our daily lives, we may know this on some level, but we may not know how to work toward bringing about such an equal distribution of resources as would be needed for freedom, justice and peace.

We can start out small by looking at our own lives. We have more control over what we give than over what we receive, but we also have control over what we receive. If we are giving in ways that are unequal, of our time, attention, affection and resources, we can make an adjustment knowing that, in so doing, we will be giving more in line with what creates harmony. If we are receiving in ways that are unequal, we can work to give more. We might take some guidance from the veins. When we look at the veins in the body, we see that they distribute to all parts of the body, treating each part as equally worthy of having its essential needs met. The brain, heart, and nerves work to distribute in ways that give and receive from head to toe, leaving no part out. So too, we can consider that there are essential requirements of individuals which need to be met.

Of course, we, as a humanity, are developing systems and processes to deliver from one part of the world to another more rapidly than ever before. But there is more work to be done.

And the new call for individuals in wealthy countries is to step up to the new challenges and opportunities. Think of five ways in which you, personally, can give more time and attention to how to bring about more equal treatment. Is there a way you can give up something and give it to another? How often do you clean out your drawers and closets and give to Goodwill or a similar organization? Can you give a meal to a local food bank? Can you download an app from Google called One Today, where a cause will be sent to your phone daily, increasing your awareness, and where you will be able to give one dollar to a new cause, on a regular basis? Can you help a local entrepreneur in some way, knowing that one of the challenges today is for small businesses to compete with global companies (an inequality)? Can you donate something to a school in an underprivileged neighborhood? You can go to DonorsChoose.org to see numerous possibilities for how you can help bring resources to schools in need. And, another way to foster equality, ask yourself if you can you write a petition to gain support for a change that would foster more balance and harmony.

If you have more materially, including a better education, than many others in the world, you might find that in fostering more equal treatment you will receive back equal treatment in ways that you may not expect: you may be regarded more highly,

BEING EQUAL

you may be respected more, you may feel better about yourself and your life. In other words, pursuing equality, may actually increase, not only the harmony in your life, but also, your happiness. As we've noted, often society today thinks or suggests that pursuing material possessions is the way to achieve happiness, but many find that by pursuing more equal treatment, we give up our want for more, and in so doing find greater fulfillment and happiness.

16

Being Free

"For to be free is not merely to cast off one's chains, but to live in a way that respects and enhances the freedom of others."

- Nelson Mandela

BEING FREE

Body part: Lungs (for venting and voicing)

Lungs are to the Body
as Freedom is to Harmonious Action,
in that both, the lungs and freedom, involve venting and voicing.

The healthy lungs vent out carbon dioxide and vent oxygen to the heart to enrich the blood. And the lungs, by venting air past the vocal chords, allow us to speak.

Freedom serves a similar purpose. It allows us to speak and share in ways that enrich lives. Speaking and acting freely, we create the necessary air, or space, that lives need to breathe or grow.

Though we, as individuals, may feel, largely, free, we may not be as free as we want to be. We might amend what Thomas Jefferson said, "The tree of liberty must be refreshed from time to time with the blood of patriots and tyrants." Better to refresh the tree of liberty by sharing in healthy ways, expelling toxins, and sharing oxygen, sharing in nourishing ways. Freedom, being expressed in unhealthy ways, includes, for example, conveying destructive words or sentiments. Freedom expressed in healthy ways lifts others up and expands the conversation.

Dialog that is healthy and constructive is that which involves a search to learn and grow. It is nourishing. By contrast, dialog which is unhealthy is not constructive and hampers healthy growth. Unkind or hurtful words, idle conversation, these impede healthy growth.

Thus, it's necessary to integrate one's use of freedom with caring, or loving behavior, much as the healthy lung is well integrated with the heart. The lung and the heart work together, so too, our voicing can work together with our effort to be loving. The saying, "if you don't have anything nice to say don't say anything at all" makes the point. And we should recognize the power of the word. As the earliest version of an oft repeated phrase goes: "The word is mightier than the sword," that by the Assyrian sage, Ahiqar, 500 BC, later offered by Euripides, as "the tongue is mightier than the blade" 400 BC, and then by the English author, Edward Bulwer-Lytton, as "the pen is mightier than the sword." Today we might say "the keyboard is mightier than the trigger." Of course, all these notions require that we make use of the power of our voice to connect with caring thought and a desire to create constructive growth and change.

Are we acting as freely in our daily lives as we would like? Are we using our freedom wisely? Are there those close to us with whom we cannot share our hopes, dreams and most meaningful desires? Are there those close to us with whom we cannot share how we feel about this or that which is important to our sense of connection in the relationship? Are we able to speak up at work? Or, is our voice thwarted in some way?

Often what keeps us unfree, in some way, is our own self-limiting fear. It takes courage, often, to speak out in ways that are constructive and fulfilling. It may take practicing how to be assertive, not aggressive or passive.

We can look at learning to become freer as we would taking a breath in and a breath out. It's something simple and deliberate we can do. Take a deep breath, let it out. This is similar to what it takes sometimes to become free of either a self-imposed or other-imposed limit on us. Let our "breath in" be one which fills us with courage and our "breath out" be one which fills others with constructive information for their growth and ours. We have the power to do this.

We can change our work, we can change our relationship, we can change our habits, simply by taking control of our freedom to feel, do and act in line with our desires for constructive change and more harmonious relationships.

17

Meeting Life's Essentials

"One cannot think well, love well, sleep well, if one has not dined well."

- Virginia Woolf

MEETING LIFE'S ESSENTIALS

Body part: Cells (for assimilating)

Cells are to the Body

as meeting Life's essentials is to creating Harmonious Action,

in that both, cells and meeting life's essentials, involve assimilating the essentials necessary for life.

Meeting our need for food, water, shelter, heat and electricity (life's essentials), involves assimilating ourselves into the world, and assimilating our needed resources into the body. Much as the cell assimilates all that is needed for life, we too, must assimilate all that we need for life.

The whole physiological functioning of the human body is built upon the foundation of the cell. Similarly, the whole behavioral functioning of the human life is built upon the foundation of the life's basic essentials.

So important are our basic life's essentials that we naturally work toward obtaining them. We take jobs we might not otherwise take, for example, simply to have these needs met. Sometimes, fear of not having these life's essentials will lead us to do many things that don't make us, or others, happy.

But we, also, sometimes, put our happiness needs above our need for life's essentials. We may indulge in activities that are fun but which are not essential, or meaningful. That is, they don't provide lasting or significant value.

The goal is to balance our need for life's essentials with our need for deeper meaningful happiness. Much as there is a tension between life and liberty, captured famously by Patrick Henry's "Give me liberty or give me death," there is a tension between our need for life's essentials and for short-term happiness — it might be looked at as being similar to the tension between needing healthy food and wanting dessert. We may not want to eat the healthy food but it's best if we find a balance between eating healthy foods and enjoying some dessert. The same could be said of striking a balance between working for our life's essential needs and our need for short-term happiness.

Many of us can have our life's essentials needs met fairly readily, but achieving happiness is much harder. And so what may happen is that we continue down the path that helps us to satisfy our life's essential needs, working at something unsatisfying, making more and more money, and then we try to use that money to buy happiness.

But the path of developing happiness can't be bought. It, often, requires us to give up the fear of not having our life's essentials needs met. It requires us to engage in service of others in meaningful ways. Most meaningful, is providing for the life's essential needs of others. How do we know they are the most meaningful? Because most, if not all of us, would rate having our life's essentials as high, if not the highest on our list of what we value or need first and foremost.

Service to others in this area, sometimes involves giving material assistance, and sometimes involves teaching others to be able to do for themselves.

It may be hard to appreciate the value of the basic essentials. Those who don't spend much time thinking about their own life's essentials, or those of others, may take them for granted. How often do you say to yourself that you are grateful for something very small and basic? For example, have you ever looked at a tube of toothpaste and stopped to be thankful that you had the money to buy it? It's a bit of an odd example but someone who has struggled may be able to relate.

What may keep some from caring about all the world's people, and their need for life's essentials, is that for those who have had an easy time of things, it's easy to think that those who go without deserve it. And perhaps, there is justice in all situations, and yet, we who have needs met can have mercy for others.

If you find yourself, or someone thinking that way, consider how mercy plays into dealing with others whom one believes deserves their misfortune — an unfortunate thought, but one that nonetheless, exists (it's at the root of the belief in survival of the fittest or social Darwinism). Mercy is defined as "compassion or forgiveness shown toward someone whom it is within one's power to punish or harm."[30] To appreciate this, think of how you might, instead of punishing a child, instruct, or inform, a child to teach them. You have the power to punish a child, but you also have the capability to lovingly teach a child. Often, instruction and information is all that is necessary to change behavior. And what a parent who instructs or informs a child, instead of punishing them, often learns is that the reason for a "bad" behavior is something other than what they thought it was. In such an approach to teaching the child the parent learns something valuable about what it means to be loving and to be loved.

We can extend this point out to suggest that there are systemic causes for difficulties that many people face, and so, rather than thinking that all people deserve the results of those systemically caused problems, we might all benefit from giving instruction and information to lift others up.

CREATING HARMONY

One of the biggest systemic problems is the inequity that causes many children in the world to be undereducated or underfed. Often, it is the case that political systems are corrupt or hegemonic, meaning that a dominant group exerts pressure or influence over the less powerful group. Hindsight shows us that often the criteria used for justifying domination over others are improper: gender, race, physical strength, etc. Today, there is still a lot of systemic priority placed on, or favor given to, "physical strength." Today's systemic benefits to the mighty are not like those of the past, whereby individuals used physical strength to rule. But there are still several examples where "physical might" dictates the opportunities a person has. For example, how a child gets educated involves some amount of "physical might." One of the most obvious examples is where wealth is attained by outer beauty, not inner beauty, and such determines the quality of education a child receives. There is a cultural norm that promotes outer beauty, which can be seen in television, movies, magazine covers, and all sorts of product sales. Such promotes the idea that outer beauty is superior to inner beauty. It's a form of physical might that we have a choice whether or not to value.

This is only one example of how the system creates dominance based on criteria which is not rooted in deep values, and yet, many of us ignore this reality.

Another example helps make the point. Often, diplomats and politicians will make the point when they take a military action, or wage a war, that they have no animosity toward the people of the country they are at war with, and that it is the leadership of the country which is unjust. And yet, inevitably, innocent lives will be taken in such situations. The point, here, is that lives can be affected by the dominance of one group over another group, and it is very hard, even when your side is in the "right" to mete out justice in a calibrated way. One need only look at how hard it is to teach, without a punishment, a child you love, to see that countries, too, must be very careful in using force to deal with bad behavior.

While this example will resonate with some people, it may not with others, and so, you can think of your own examples where you see injustice in the world to recognize that there are plenty of opportunities for offering mercy and compassion for the difficulties people face.

You don't want to be on the side of either the dominant and unjust force or the weaker side, and yet, much of whether you are or not is a factor of where you were born, and whether the system is one where right makes right, not might makes right. So, to avoid being part of the collective oppressor, or oppressed, it is incumbent upon you to remake your world and your system, to find places where you can help those who don't have their life's essentials met, and who don't have the opportunity to have their life's essentials met.

It may require a major change in your priorities and values. But don't be overwhelmed or dissuaded to act by the thought that you cannot make a difference. It all adds up, and even small steps make a difference. Of course, at the other end of the spectrum, don't fall into the thinking that doing a small amount is all you can do, or that giving one percent is enough. You can start small, but set your sights on making your whole life about developing your talents to help "the least among us"—we're all equal—and you will find that you will experience more happiness and harmony.

18

Putting It All Together: Behaviors and Values

PUTTING IT ALL TOGETHER: BEHAVIORS AND VALUES

Certainly, we have not gone into depth into direct solutions about how we can become freer from the challenges that generally stand in people's way, such as becoming free from a limiting job or relationship, or into depth about direct solutions to global problems, including how to end hunger, homelessness, poverty, or war.

What, instead, we have suggested is that by focusing on freeing ourselves of insensitivity, thoughtlessness, unresponsiveness, and so on, we actually become empowered to take specific steps that fit our situation and challenge. When we free ourselves of fear-based behaviors, such as greed, anger and selfishness, we become freer to be our true, and more loving, self. And it is then that we begin to free ourselves from the "bad" boss or partner, and it is then that we find more and more solutions that reduce lack and conflict. This is because harmonious behaviors lead to unexpected solutions that are ultimately freeing.

The gifts of our loving behaviors that we exchange through our aligned actions are the ones that create healthier and more powerful bonds.

We actually have the freedom to do them—they are free, they cost nothing. Connecting with this limitless freedom, engaging in life thoughtfully, lovingly, and aligned, we find there's even more excitement, enticement, enthusiasm and empowerment.

Recognizing that equality is an essential value to promote, we also recognize that our happiness is bound up with the happiness of others.[31]

To make the point of how our happiness can be bound up with the happiness of all others, consider the example, albeit a stark one, of people who go to school, a restaurant, work, or a movie theater to enjoy themselves, and how their life is changed if it becomes the setting for a violent crime. Though on a percentage basis these types of events are rare, there are innumerous acts of harm committed by individuals which then interfere with others' happiness. When one's life and happiness is affected by the crime of another, one quickly realizes that one's own happiness and freedom can be affected by the lack of happiness and lack of respect for life by another. Of course, we see it in less extreme ways also. We see it in work, or personal, situations where we may not be treated as an equal, or where we may not be free to follow our passions, and live purposefully. A sense of fulfillment and deep happiness can only be experienced when one is treated as an equal and one treats others as equals.

We can create happiness by treating others as equals in simple, but important ways. We can give family members, or workers, the opportunity to share their voices and feelings. We can give one another equal time and attention. We can share all our resources equally with all those whom we love and all those whom we impact, which in a highly interconnected world, becomes really all, the whole world. Our choices, and actions have far-reaching effects.

That our true happiness and freedom is bound up with that of others close to us is somewhat easy to see. But that it is also bound up with the true happiness and freedom of those in a foreign land may be harder to see. Martin Luther King, Jr. makes this point well when he so eloquently connected his children's lives to others' lives, and their happiness to others' happiness: "I said to my children, 'I'm going to work and do everything that I can do to see that you get a good education. I don't ever want you to forget that there are millions of God's children who will not and cannot get a good education, and I don't want you feeling that you are better than they are. For you will never be what you ought to be until they are what they ought to be."

PUTTING IT ALL TOGETHER: BEHAVIORS AND VALUES

To move to this state where we achieve the happiness that comes from regarding other's lives as equal to our own, we can ask ourselves: Are we truly happy when we live lavishly while also aware that a person in Ethiopia is starving to death? Well, many people try to minimize their knowledge, and while ignorance may be bliss, it does not yield the fulfillment that comes with moving beyond one's most inner circles, to love more completely.

Most of us realize that if the person starving in another country was right next to us, we would not be truly happy. Technological advances can help bring that person closer to us, both to recognize the problem and to resolve it.

But, many of us respond to technology and a culture that promotes wealth and consumption in ways that move us farther away from one another. We may want more of what we can have for ourselves, such as the newer technology for entertainment. The result is that we become less caring about the larger world.

As we move further and further into a world and culture bombarded with sensationalism, restless activity, and other harmful influences, our ability to connect with one another in loving ways becomes numbed.[32] We may think we can love the one closest to us fully, while completely ignoring the one on the other side of the world, but if we do that, we underutilize our full potential, and so we fall short and our love falls short.

When we don't fight against these tensions and draws, or temptations, we lose touch with our deeper selves and our most intimate selves. We lose touch with the full power of love, to fill others up, and to fill ourselves up. Adam Smith feared the "numbness of the mind" that might come with industrialism, and thus he advocated education for all as an antidote.[33] And society is becoming more and more educated in science, math and technology, for example. Perhaps, it's time for a broad-reaching education of the heart, whereby we share, with others, empowering behaviors and values.

Teaching these, one imagines, becomes increasingly important as global sized problems and threats present themselves. The actions of a relative few executives at banks and investment companies led to economic challenges for many millions in 2008, and carry on, for many, still today, for those in the United States and around the world. For example, in Spain, unemployment in those under age twenty-five is fifty-six percent, the effects of those acts still being felt.[34] There are, of course, other important examples, of global sized problems: pollution in China can harm the United States; it knows no boundaries. Unfair wages or working conditions in India exploits Indian workers and can cost jobs in the United States. Again, excessive financial gains for one (the few) at the expense of others, ultimately, is harmful for all, both for the oppressed and the oppressor.

And, so, to address these problems, we can look for tangible solutions, but even before we do, we can begin to make our own actions more sensitive and equal, and we can begin to make our own actions more thoughtful regarding the impacts on others.

We may not know in every situation what love would require, but we can more readily recognize what the sensitive, thoughtful, responsive act would be when we make it a point to learn to develop these qualities.

Narrowing the inequalities in our world, and reducing harmful behavior and exploitation, begins by healing the disparities within ourselves and those closest to us. We can do the best for ourselves and others by "moving into" a better balance, desiring more equality in our own hearts and minds. Those things that are imbalanced outside in the world start with the imbalances inside ourselves. A system whose "heart" is based on greed and fear is one born from the greed and fear that lives inside each of us.

We can look at the system as a person, with an ego, with all the same problems as our egos: judgment, pride, jealousy, greed, anger, fear and other harmful emotions. By working with ourselves and befriending our own shadows, we can begin moving beyond the limitations of our own unconscious, or unaware, commitment to inequality.

No one likes to look at the greed, fear, anger, or jealousy in their own heart, but we all have or have had one or more of these emotions at some time in our life.

Looking at ourselves honestly requires effort and attention, and a longing to grow toward love and more loving ways of living. To change the system "out there," we begin by working on our own hearts. This takes courage, sensitivity, thoughtfulness, and love toward one self and others. Patiently, with commitment and dedication, we heal these imbalances on the inside, and we begin to slowly and steadily act in more balanced ways on the outside. Inwardly, we reflect, and outwardly we act more lovingly, more authentically, more harmoniously, more equally. Equality within ourselves leads to equality in the world we see.

Life's essentials, such as, food, water, safety and health are the basic needs we all share. And when we focus, with loving intention, on achieving true happiness, and respecting the needs of others, life essentials get delivered in the process. Positive transformation begins within us, stems out from us, and, positively, reaches others.

When we don't purchase excessively, we have more for what we most need and more for what others most need. For example,

CREATING HARMONY

when we give up excessive dinners out, or overindulgences in shopping, we have more for base essential needs. In the process, we induce society to make decisions that reinforce those more balanced choices.

We may not think that we can influence behavior with our purchases but we can and do. The reduction in the use of trans fats in foods was in response to public reaction to their use and adverse health effects. The offering by many grocery stores of reusable bags was in response to the need to reduce paper and plastic usage. The switch, years ago, by McDonalds from foam to paper for their hamburger boxes, and more recently for their hot cups, was also a response to the public.[35] While there is considerably more to do, the lesson is clear: our behaviors and actions matter.

More and more, we see the realization, by many, of the importance of satisfying needs not wants. Even in schools, we are seeing children being taught about needs versus wants. It's simple economics, or said differently, it's the economics of love: when we give up the extra television show, there's less advertising dollars for those companies which may not be aligned with deeper values. When we buy or rent a movie such as *Food Inc.*, or *The Corporation*, and not something sensational, we send a message to Hollywood that we value values more, in and from one another, and sensational entertainment less.

When we let go of the pursuit of those experiences which result in feelings of lack, or emptiness, and we engage more in those which foster harmony and peace, we generate more interest from others in fostering these high ideals. We wind up prioritizing life's essentials over excessive or wanton needs.

When we change our values in such a way, we transform a world which has abundance for the few into a world which delivers the needs of all. The world today produces enough food and water to supply all of the world's population. We simply need to get it to the world.

We can say no to waste and environmentally damaging behavior in our own lives, and the corporations will follow. We can say no to greed, and the movies and trendsetters will follow. We can say no to the high paying but immoral jobs, and those jobs will go away. We can say no to a hierarchical system that values worth based on predominately quantifiable financial measures, rather than predominately on the qualitative values of true happiness, freedom, equality and life's essentials, which are immeasurable.

In summary, true happiness comes from within. It comes from making the *free* choice to foster *each other's happiness* and each other's *health and safety*. Such happiness radiates outward. One gives up thinking of happiness as something one takes in and recognizes happiness as an experience of giving. In this experience, one recognizes that happiness does not belong to one self, and one falls into a formless, expansive, and loving experience. And, in so doing, one gains everything because one has moved into harmony with one's best nature.

Again, but now, with greater clarity as to what it means, in line with the golden rule, our shared needs of life, liberty, the pursuit of happiness, and equality combine into *Hope for All*: **H**appiness **O**f **P**ursuit, **E**quality **for A L**iberated **L**ife, a beautiful phrase and a loving acronym for children and adults, alike, to share. We can see *Hope for All* as a loving notion, representative of four undeniable ideals, realizable as we work toward making ourselves more harmonious and more wholly aligned.

CREATING HARMONY

PART TWO

BEYOND BEHAVIORS AND VALUES

If you are like most people, who have gotten to this point, you probably feel like there's a lot for you to digest.

And so, you might wonder why there's more.

Well, as with most discoveries, one discovery leads to another and another. Or, to extensions, and further applications.

And, also, it leads to more questions.

This next part addresses some fascinating extensions and in the process addresses several questions. It shows how we might consider attitudes and character traits as being different than behaviors, but also important. It shows how we might consider how this insight applies to our societal framework, of institutions. Can we map our society according to the body? That's what we found is also possible. And lastly, we thought it important to share how we might take this approach further, by recognizing that there are several other valuable behavioral traits which also can be compared to parts of the body which we have not mentioned to this point.

19

Beyond Behaviors: Attitudes

BEYOND BEHAVIORS: ATTITUDES

To this point, we've focused on nine key behaviors and four values: Aligned Action, Love, Thoughtfulness, Responsiveness, Unity, Individuality, Sensitivity, Meaningfulness, Empathy, Life, Liberty, Happiness and Equality.

We have not yet, in this book, considered whether attitudes and character traits are also of value for harmony and balanced interactions, and how they differ from behavioral traits.

Some say that our attitudes are what we experience on the inside and behaviors are what we exhibit on the outside. And some say that our character is different than our attitudes and behaviors in that it is made up of both our attitude and our behavior. This is a view we also take. If it is true that attitude is different than behavior, and that character is also different than behavior, it makes sense that we would want to look at some attitude and character traits that might relate to creating harmony, in addition to the behavioral traits.

So, we've selected one attitude trait and one character trait for each behavior trait. Each attitude and character trait chosen is one which closely relates to a behavioral trait. In this chapter, we'll look at attitudes, and in the next chapter, we'll look at character traits.

The importance of considering our inner attitudes is that often we may change an outer behavior, but inwardly not feel good or right. By developing our attitude, we actually harmonize our inner experience with our outer behavior.

So, in this chapter, we'll take a look at nine attitudes which we think are as essential as the behavioral traits.

CREATING HARMONY

Attitude	Behavior
Attuned	Aligned action
Loyal	Loving
Thankful	Thoughtful
Respectful	Responsive
Understanding	Uniting
Independent	Individualizing
Sympathetic	Sensitive
Mutual	Meaningful
Embracing	Empathy

BEYOND BEHAVIORS: ATTITUDES

Attuned

Though it's not a word most of us, likely, give much thought to, attunement, being attuned, is an important attitude. And not only don't we think about it, we probably do not know much about what it means. Being attuned, in our attitude, we "bring into harmony" (or tune)[36] our attitude and our actions. Attuned, we are more fully aware.

We want to become more aware of our inner attitude and we also want to make our attitude aligned with our actions. Attuned, we are not thinking one thing on the inside and acting inconsistently on the outside. It is not that we necessarily need to change our action—it may be that we need to change our attitude on the inside.

To say we want to become attuned, or that we want to become more aware, begs the question, how exactly do we become more attuned and aware. One way to do this is to recognize that becoming attuned and aware is done by developing several attitudes, such as being loyal, thankful, and the several others we're going to describe. Though it is a partial list, it is an important list for not only getting in touch with what is going on inside us, but also for making what is going on inside us positive and constructive so that we can more easily succeed at creating harmony, not only with others, but also with ourselves.

Loyalty

We can think, next, about how to develop a loyal attitude. A loyal attitude is the basis for loving behavior. With an attitude of loyalty we are more able to be loving. When we set a goal to be loyal to one we love, we make it easier for ourselves to be loving.

And it helps us to feel more aligned, and more in sync with our best self.

If we need the reminder, by reminding ourselves regularly to be loyal, we move ourselves to a place where our inner eye is directed more faithfully, and our outer eye can follow.

When we are loyal, we create more loving energy outward and more loving energy comes back. When we refer to love, we're referring not only to love in our relationships, but also to the broader humanity.

When we ask ourselves, if we do, why we ought to be loyal to those who might be far away, and foreign to us, as G.K. Chesterton well said, "We are all in the same boat, in a stormy sea, and we owe each other a terrible loyalty." Chesterton speaks of loyalty in a storm. And as the reformation's Martin Luther notes, "Where the battle rages, there the loyalty of the soldier is proved." And so it is with all of us, as soldiers in our own lives. It is in the difficult times, when the challenges arise, that we must focus on being loyal to those closest to us and to the broader humanity.

Thankful

To become more attuned and more loyal, we can develop an attitude of thankfulness. An attitude of thankfulness involves, of course, giving thanks for what we have. As Oprah Winfrey says, "Be thankful for what you have; you'll end up having more. If you concentrate on what you don't have, you will never, ever have enough." What you will have more of when you are thankful for what you have is more fulfillment, more of a sense of satisfaction.

Whatever the mind focuses on affects how we feel. Look at your life, and give thanks for three things, three things people have done for you, and three things you have done for others. Holding this attitude in your heart and mind regularly, you will feed your ability to be loyal to love.

Consider this story about the value of being thankful. The story is titled, Attention to the Smallest Detail. It's a story about a janitor ... and more.

A lady worked as a janitor in a company for many years.

Now being a janitor is a pretty thankless job, which many of us might consider as a "dirty" job or at least pretty far down the totem pole. In other words, probably not a whole lot of fun.

It happened the company changed owners. Within a few days, the new owner wrote a personal thank you card to every employee in the company. He had his assistant go around and hand them out.

When this lady received and opened her card, she burst into tears. She asked if she could be excused from work. Thinking she was sick, she was allowed leave for the rest of the day.

What Really Happened.

What the story was — they found out a few days later — she had never received even a verbal thank you from the previous owners and management — much less a personal card.

And she had worked there 20 or 30 years!

So she was really touched when the new owner sent her a card of appreciation.

And ... she had been thinking the change of ownership was probably a good time to quit.

And ... she was planning to let them know that very day.

Which she didn't. Because the little time, the little extra effort of the owner to send a little business thank you card, helped the lady change her mind.[37]

Clearly, giving thanks in our attitude, naturally, can extend out not only into a thankful act, but into a thoughtful act — and that is what the new owners in that story did. And as G.K. Chesterton said, "Thanks are the highest form of thought."

Respect

Underlying our ability for thankfulness, often, is an attitude of respect. Respect is defined as "a feeling of deep admiration for someone or something elicited by their abilities, qualities, or achievements."[38] To be clear, respect, inherent in that last story, goes much further than admiring abilities and achievements, as is reflected in this further definition: "a feeling of admiring someone or something that is good, valuable, important, etc." These are qualities apart from the achievements which are typically awarded, such as for excelling in material ways, or in the sports and entertainment fields.

Often we might value someone more by how much they achieve, it may lead us to respect a president more than a janitor. Apparently, that might have been the case with the first owner of that company, in the last story, who hadn't given the janitor so much as a thank you in all those years. Respect that is based on whether someone or something "is good" might lead us to value someone who lives with values and lives a virtuous life, irrespective of their occupation or level of material achievement.

BEYOND BEHAVIORS: ATTITUDES

While that may seem obvious, we might recognize that often, in society, we tend to take someone's ability to live virtuously for granted, or we may even assume it — we may assume it based upon their participation in a church or a giving, caring organization. But perhaps, good advice for young people who are evaluating a life partner might be to value less the vocation one's partner is intent on pursuing or engaged in and to value more the qualities and behaviors that the individual exhibits.

Ask yourself daily whether you are showing those whom you love respect. And if not, it may be because you are not understanding aspects of them, or of yourself, which takes us to the next attitude.

Understanding

To respect others, we have to understand others. For that matter, to respect ourselves we also need to understand ourselves. And sometimes understanding another, and why they are behaving the way they are, it might be that we need to better understand our role in the "dance." By the dance, we mean the interactional challenge that we may have with another.

An understanding attitude is one which seeks to see the truth of a situation, and seeks to recognize the feelings that another is experiencing, or that you yourself are experiencing. As one saying goes, *be curious not furious*. With an understanding attitude, we are open and receptive to what another needs and we can more easily unify to meet our own needs and those of others. John Steinbeck said it well when he said, "Try to understand men. If you understand each other you will be kind to each other. Knowing a man well never leads to hate and almost always leads to love."

CREATING HARMONY

Remind yourself when you are frustrated or furious to question whether you fully understand the situation. Likely, you don't. And if you think you do, likely if you are frustrated or furious, you don't, because with understanding we tend to feel better. We recognize what is causing the bad behavior in another and we understand our role, if we have one, and what we can do to change the dance, to change the music, to change the venue... to change the timing... there are so many things we can change to adjust and improve, once we achieve understanding.

Here is a story about understanding.

"One of the famous characteristics of goats is their irritability. I don't know if it's true of all goats, but it's certainly true of mountain goats in the Rockies. These goats are so prickly that if they stay in close proximity they not only hurt each other, but have even been known to kill their neighbour.

As puzzling as this behaviour may seem to us, there is a good reason for it. Mountain goats live in areas where there is a very limited food supply. If they were to live in groups they'd all end up dying as none would get enough to eat.

It can be the same with people. Often their behaviour is puzzling to us, sometimes downright offensive. They can be cold, prickly, irritable and harsh. Yet if we take the time to look we'll find that there are usually reasons why people are like this — perhaps they've been hurt themselves, perhaps they're dealing with great stresses. But whatever the reason there is a reason for their prickliness. Unlike goats however, it's not healthy for us humans to live apart, and perhaps we need to explore our own prickliness and reach out lovingly to those who are so prickly."[39]

BEYOND BEHAVIORS: ATTITUDES

Certainly, understanding why someone is irritable, abrasive, unkind... is a good start. We would simply add to the story that if your human friend is actually a mountain goat, then you might just have to give them the space that a mountain goat needs. Nonetheless, make sure that you understand the friend well, and understand enough about yourself, before you write them off as a mountain goat.

Independence

One goal, as part of harmonizing, is to achieve interdependence, a state where you are mutually and equally dependent upon one another — such is a state where all are irreplaceable and valued. Part of achieving this is achieving independence. Independence and dependence creates interdependence.

When we hold an independent attitude, we believe in our ability to contribute in a unique, valuable and significant way to others. And we believe in our ability to act with integrity — we believe that we can become independent of succumbing to amoral and immoral demands, and to harmful temptations.

And this type of independence allows us to act in ways which are positively and constructively individualizing. For example, one is not drawn to follow the crowd when the crowd is going the wrong way; one is drawn to lead people in the right direction.

The Christmas story, *Santa Claus is Comin' to Town*, we may not think of as championing the importance of individuality, and yet, that is a big part of the story. This excerpt makes the point. This is the discussion between the head elf and Hermey, the elf who wants to be a dentist in the North Pole.

CREATING HARMONY

Head Elf: Hermey! Aren't you finished painting that yet? There's a pile up a mile wide behind you! What's eating you, boy?

Hermey: Not happy with my work, I guess.

Head Elf: What?

Hermey: I just don't like to make toys.

Head Elf: Oh well if that's all... What? You don't like to make toys?

Hermey: Nnno.

Head Elf: [to the other elves] Hermey doesn't like to make toys!

Elves: [whispering to each other] Hermey doesn't like to make toys. Shame on you!

Head Elf: Do you mind telling me what you do want to do?

Hermey: Well, sir, someday, I'd like to be a... a dentist.

Head Elf: A - dentist?

Hermey: Well, we need one up here. I've been studying. It's fascinating; you've no idea. Molars and bicuspids and incisors...

Head Elf: [interrupts] Now listen, you: you're an elf, and elves make toys. Now, get to work!

[whistle blows]

Head Elf: Ten minute break!

[Hermey smiles, but then the head elf jumps him]

BEYOND BEHAVIORS: ATTITUDES

Head Elf: Not for you! Finish the job, or you're fired!

Later, this is the discussion Hermey has with Rudolph, as Rudolph joins him.

Hermey: Hey, what do you say we both be independent together, huh?

Rudolph: You wouldn't mind my - red nose?

Hermey: Not if you don't mind me being a dentist.

Rudolph: [shaking hands with Hermey] It's a deal.

There is something about this story that connects with many of us, and yet, much of the world does not support us acting like Hermey and Rudolph, who himself, joined Hermey in becoming independent. In fact, most of the world is like the Head Elf telling people that they have to make toys. Hermey's change began with an independent attitude. It led him to be fired. Rudolph's change began with a difference, the red nose, which led him to have to either hide his individuality or run away from those who ridiculed him. It was an independent attitude that led each of them to act in ways that were individualizing.

Ask yourself where you would like to be expressing your individuality more, and how you can develop a more independent attitude to help you become more individualizing—remember, do this with the goal of becoming more interdependent — in other words, the goal is to channel this attitude to becoming more loving, and more mutual, not more isolated, or alone.

CREATING HARMONY

Sympathizing

In an effort to improve our ability to connect with all others, those closest to us and those afar, we can develop our sense of sympathy for others. It is common to have sympathy for individuals who suffer a grave loss, or for those who are sick or have suffered in some significant and noticeable way. If we see a starving child, or a soldier seriously wounded or killed, or a suffering mom, we will naturally, have immediate sympathy. It's harder to feel sympathy for another, however, when someone does something harmful to us. And yet, we want to extend our sympathy to all whom we are affected by and to all whom we affect. Adopting this attitude recognizes that one definition of sympathy is "an affinity, association, or relationship between persons or things wherein whatever affects one similarly affects the other."[40] In other words, it recognizes that we're all connected.

Beyond feeling for the feelings of another, and beyond recognizing that we are all one, having sympathy also means to be in "unity or harmony in action or effect,"[41] as in "in complete sympathy with the scheme as a whole."[42] In other words, being in sympathy, in one meaning of the word, means to be in agreement with the actions of another. Trying to harmonize with others involves trying to achieve this kind of sympathy.

To achieve this degree of sympathy with another's actions takes work. It requires us to recognize where someone's action, or aims, and our own actions, or aims, are either at odds or in agreement. And it requires us to work at resolving the areas of disagreement or disjointedness. In a situation where we are at odds with another, it may be that we have to reduce or eliminate our involvement if we cannot reconcile the differences, but often we can work at bettering our understanding of the differences and with effort, resolve them.

We can ask whether we are sympathizing with the day-to-day challenges that another in our life faces. If we are having a challenge with someone, we can try to sympathize with what frustrates them, what challenges them, and what concerns them.

We can also sympathize with what they like, as well. Sympathy extends, not only to the down emotions, such as sadness and sorrow, but also to the up emotions, such as happiness and joy. We can learn to embrace what others find pleasurable and in so doing we become in sympathy with them. It may seem natural to do this, but often we do not meet another with a positive emotion when the opportunity presents itself. We may be caught up in a down state when another is sharing something that could lift us up. Often, someone else's good feelings can be so easy to share and facilitate.

The reason for sympathy's harmonizing, and frankly, transformative effects can be understood quite simply by recognizing the philosopher David Hume's point that approval is pleasure and disapproval pain or uneasiness.[43] None of us like to be disapproved of, and all of us like to be approved of. Sympathizing we are able to approve of another, at least, in part, and then, move them where they may need growth or loving teaching, or, move ourselves where we need growth. Resisting another's feelings we create an impediment to growth; sympathizing we create an opening for growth.

Mutuality

CREATING HARMONY

All of the attitudes we've mentioned reflect a goal of mutuality, but it can help to think specifically about developing an attitude of mutuality.

An attitude of mutuality sees others as mutually worthy of respect, apart from another's failings. It puts our oneness ahead of our separateness. It puts being humane ahead of being first, better, or in any way superior. Many of the world's problems, and the challenges in individual lives, stem from the idea that "one is superior to another and thus, deserve more." A notion that says, "one is superior to another and thus more responsible" is different than one that says, "one is superior to another and thus deserves more" — that is, all, regardless of societal position are seen as equally worthy and deserving, at least of life's essentials.

When we cultivate an attitude of mutuality we aim to strike mutually supportive agreements. We aim to exchange equal value. We aim to recognize the deeper needs of all.

Dr. Judith Jordan describes the importance of mutuality, in a paper titled, *The Meaning of Mutuality*: "Crucial to a mature sense of mutuality is an appreciation of the wholeness of the other person with a special awareness of the other's subjective experience."[44] She adds, "Through empathy, and an active interest in the other as a different, complex person, one develops the capacity at first to allow the other's differentness and ultimately to value and encourage those qualities which make that person different and unique."[45] We can remind ourselves daily to act mutually, and we can question ourselves regularly to see if we are acting in ways which are mutually respectful.

As Martin Luther King, Jr. said: "In a real sense, all life is interrelated. All people are caught in an inescapable network of mutuality, tied in a single garment of destiny." We might know this at a general level, but do we consider all those around us as of being so critical to our life? Each step we take to work toward the best for all those around us, is a step which strengthens that garment.

Embracing

To help foster all these attitudes, we can also develop an embracing attitude. An embracing attitude embraces differences. It embraces the good and bad. It embraces the ups and downs of life. It recognizes that by being embracing in our attitude, we are best able to grow and help others to grow.

In our own lives, embracing the bad as well as the good, the down as well the up, we help to transform the bad and the down. We recognize that everything happens for a reason and that we can use the challenges to grow even higher and more harmonious. Everything is an opportunity to rise and grow.

Gandhi getting thrown of the train, King being imprisoned, Rosa Parks being charged with a violation of the law, Helen Keller being deaf-blind, Beethoven losing his hearing, Lincoln losing several runs for elected office before becoming president, Thomas Jefferson and the founding fathers (and mothers) being at odds with the King of England, Galileo, asserting against the powers-that-be that the earth revolved around the sun, all these "bads," all these downs, were opportunities for good to triumph.

In our everyday lives there are bads and downs to triumph over, and changing our attitude which helps us to do so is completely within our control. We have the control over whether we see the glass as half full, half empty, or both. By bringing into our daily self-talk words such as attunement, loyalty, thankfulness, respect, understanding, independence, sympathy, mutuality, and embracing, we strengthen our ability to act in harmonious ways.

20

Beyond Attitudes and Behavior: Character

CREATING HARMONY

Attitude	Behavior	Character
Attuned	Aligned action	Authentic
Loyal	Loving	Lawful
Thankful	Thoughtful	Truthful
Respectful	Responsive	Responsible
Understanding	Uniting	Unifying
Independent	Individualizing	Integrity
Sympathetic	Sensitive	Sensible
Mutual	Meaningful	Mature
Embracing	Empathetic	Encouraging

Often it is said that the whole is greater than the sum of the parts, the idea being that the way the parts are put together leads to something new and different—and better. We might apply this to the sum of our attitudes and our behavioral traits. We might say that our attitudes and our behaviors together create a whole which we might call our character. And that character is a whole which is greater than the sum of the parts.

What this would mean is that we could identify a set of character traits which would relate to each of the attitude and behavioral traits.

Again, we've chosen words with the same beginning initial, which also relate in meaning to the several behavioral traits, to aid with remembering them. The character trait concepts chosen are ones that seem to have a close relationship to the attitude and behavior traits. For example, related to the attitude of respect and the behavior of responsiveness is the character trait being responsible. And, for example, related to the attitude of sympathy and the behavior of sensitivity is the character trait being sensible. These may seem, at first glance, to be obviously related.

Other character traits chosen may not seem to be so obviously related to the attitude and behavior trait, but upon explanation, the relationship becomes clearer. For example, the attitude of loyalty seems to relate well to the behavior of being loving, because undergirding a truly loving attitude is loyalty or fidelity to the one(s) we love. When we introduce the character trait of being lawful, we might say that it's being chosen simply because it begins with l and therefore is simply chosen to help us remember this longer list of three sets of traits. But there is actually a very important relationship between being loving and being lawful. It's that the highest laws are laws of love. That is, laws, at their best, are intended to create loving behavior. We'll develop this relationship below, as we describe each of several character traits that relate to creating attuned, aligned, and authentic interactions.

Authenticity

Authenticity is a character trait that might be seen as a pinnacle trait. When we are authentic, we are genuine and true. We are not trying to be something we are not. We are not putting on airs, or being fake. It is not a façade we are projecting but an image that is in line with our substance.

Being authentic is not, as some might think, merely being truthful, it is being "real and actual,"[46] and in that sense, actualizing.

Much as acting aligned is achievable by bringing together traits, such as being loving, thoughtful, responsive and so on in our behavior, being authentic is achievable by bringing together traits, such as being lawful, truthful and several other character traits.

Lawful

Being lawful, above, we began to describe as being related to being loving. Laws, such as the golden rule reflect the connection between law and love. One, the law, is intended to guide the other, the behavior to be loving.

Other types of laws, are informal, such as manners, mores, customs and norms. These, too, are intended to guide behavior to be loving.

We have written, throughout, that the ideals of life, liberty, happiness and equality need to be the aims of being loving, thoughtful, responsive, and so on. And, so too, these are the aims of lawfulness.

Truthful

To help us be lawful, in the best sense of this word, we can work to develop a character that is truthful. Being truthful, we are, of course, honest and sincere. Truthfulness, as Edward R. Murrow, the news broadcaster, said, has a snowball effect which impacts how we are received: "To be persuasive we must be believable; to be believable we must be credible; credible we must be truthful." And the snowball effect of being truthful is how "honest Abe" eventually became president.[47] As a store clerk, as soon as he realized he had shortchanged someone, by even pennies, he would close the store, and walk the distance to return it. He developed a reputation for honesty and it gradually built his popularity. He became sought after for mediation and adjudication of disputes. In our own lives, of course, we can probably remember how either honesty or dishonesty has served us, and we can remind ourselves that being truthful is essential for genuine and authentic connections.

Responsible

We must learn to take responsibility for our inner states. We might ask ourselves, to begin with, to whom do we owe a loyalty to? And, are we being responsible to them?

We might also look at what is keeping ourselves from being responsible, or meeting a responsibility.

If we don't feel we are being as responsible as we want to be, can we put a plan in place to improve? Try to make a list of a few simple things you might be able to do to be more responsible. Brainstorm to create possible ideas. In brainstorming, many of the ideas may not be ones you will ultimately act upon, but it may lead you to find one or two that you can act on.

In identifying where you feel responsible, be careful not to let others define your responsibilities in ways that do not allow you to be a unique individual. For example, a parent may want his or her child to become an accountant when the child wants to develop their artistic talents. Is being an accountant a responsibility of the child? Can the child do both? Or, another example, a parent may want to stay home and raise a child, where the world is pressuring the parent to work. It's up to the individual to recognize which decision is the most responsible. Another example, a boss might tell a worker that the worker needs to do something which the employee feels is unethical. Where is the responsibility?

CREATING HARMONY

Becoming responsible in a way that is fully actualizing and authentic considers all those who are affected by our choices — not only those closest to us, but those farthest from us as well. When Gandhi made salt from the sea to help free the Indian people from British rule which left many Indians poor, it was illegal, as it violated British law over India, but it was a responsible choice, as it recognized not only the right of the Indian people to self-rule, but also the responsibility to oppose an unjust law and rule.

Unifying

While uniting may bring together those of like mind and interest, unifying brings together opposing sides. We unite with others to form teams, for example; we unify to form a league. Unifying also differs from uniting, in that unifying implies reducing two into one, as in the unification of Germany, which brought East and West Germany into one whole Germany. By contrast uniting involves bringing separate entities together into one unit, while retaining their individual separateness, as in the United States.

Returning to Gandhi's example, were Gandhi to champion violence, his approach would be dividing, but where he championed civil disobedience it was unifying, in that he earned the respect of many of his English opponents.

Of course, it is hard to unify with our opponents. How many of us look at our "persecutor" and seek to unify with that person? Perhaps, most of us have, at one time or another, unified with someone who was initially opposed to us, in some way. But most, if not all, of us can work to do an even better job at unifying.

BEYOND ATTITUDES AND BEHAVIOR: CHARACTER

When we seek to act and speak in ways that are unifying, we do so with the recognition that even our opponent is connected to us, and worthy of our care.

Integrity

The character trait of integrity is closely related to unity and unification, with both those words being considered synonyms of integrity.[48] But we may think of integrity as the facet of our character which is connected to putting moral values first in our individual behavior. In *To Kill A Mockingbird*, Harper Lee said it well, when Atticus Finch says: "They're certainly entitled to think that, and they're entitled to full respect for their opinions... but before I can live with other folks I've got to live with myself. The one thing that doesn't abide by majority rule is a person's conscience." Or, as the screenwriter Lillian Hellman put it: "I cannot and will not cut my conscience to fit this year's fashions." Integrity means that while we hold an independent attitude and we act in ways that express our individuality, we do so guided to serve others.

Here is a story that highlights individuality with integrity. Ask yourself, if you would have done what Jim did or something different?

"A successful businessman was growing old and knew it was time to choose a successor to take over the business. Instead of choosing one of his directors or his children, he decided to do something different. He called all the young executives in his company together.

He said, 'It is time for me to step down and choose the next CEO. I have decided to choose one of you.' The young executives were shocked, but the boss continued, 'I am going to give each one of you a seed today—one very special seed. I want you to plant the seed, water it, and come back here one year from today with what you have grown from the seed I have given you. I will then judge the plants that you bring, and the one I choose will be the next CEO.'

One man, named Jim, was there that day and he, like the others, received a seed. He went home and excitedly, told his wife the story. She helped him get a pot, soil and compost and he planted the seed. Every day he would water it and watch to see if it had grown. After about three weeks, some of the other executives began to talk about their seeds and the plants that were beginning to grow.

Jim kept checking his seed, but nothing ever grew. Three weeks, four weeks, five weeks went by, still nothing. By now, others were talking about their plants, but Jim didn't have a plant and he felt like a failure.

Six months went by—still nothing in Jim's pot. He just knew he had killed his seed. Everyone else had trees and tall plants, but he had nothing. Jim didn't say anything to his colleagues, however, he just kept watering and fertilizing the soil. He so wanted the seed to grow.

A year went by and the CEO asked the young executives to bring their plants to work for inspection.

When Jim told his wife that he wasn't going to take an empty pot, she asked him to be honest about what happened. Jim felt sick to his stomach, it was going to be the most embarrassing moment of his life, but he knew his wife was right. He took his empty pot to the board room.

BEYOND ATTITUDES AND BEHAVIOR: CHARACTER

When Jim arrived, he was amazed at the variety of plants grown by the other executives. They were beautiful — in all shapes and sizes. Jim put his empty pot on the floor and many of his colleagues laughed, a few felt sorry for him!

When the CEO arrived, he surveyed the room and greeted his young executives. Jim just tried to hide in the back. 'My, what great plants, trees and flowers you have grown,' said the CEO. 'Today one of you will be appointed the next CEO!'

All of a sudden, the CEO spotted Jim at the back of the room with his empty pot. He asked Jim to come to the front of the room. Jim was terrified. He thought, 'The CEO knows I'm a failure! Maybe he will have me fired!'

When Jim got to the front, the CEO asked him what had happened to his seed. Jim told him the story. The CEO asked everyone to sit down except Jim. He looked at Jim, and then announced to the young executives, 'Behold your next Chief Executive Officer—Jim!'

Jim couldn't believe it. Jim couldn't even grow his seed. 'How could he be the new CEO?' the others said.

Then the CEO said, 'One year ago today, I gave everyone in this room a seed. I told you to take the seed, plant it, water it, and bring it back to me today. But I gave you all boiled seeds; they were dead—it was not possible for them to grow.

All of you, except Jim, have brought me trees and plants and flowers. When you found that the seed would not grow, you substituted another seed for the one I gave you. Jim was the only one with the courage and honesty to bring me a pot with my seed in it. Therefore, he is the one who will be the new Chief Executive Officer!'"[49]

Sensible

With a sympathetic attitude, and sensitive behavior, we can be guided to act sensibly, meaning with good sense or judgment. Being sensible in our character, we see what is "perceptible to the senses or to reason or understanding" and connect to it at a feeling level, thereby integrating our ability for sensitivity with our ability for reason and understanding.

Mature

We go beyond being mutual, in our attitude, and meaningful, in our behavior, to become mature in our character. By mature we mean "having or showing the mental and emotional qualities of an adult," or "having reached a final or desired state." With fulfillment as an aim, there must be some sense of being guided toward completion.

Encouraging

And in developing our character we must capture the energizing state of being encouraging. Embracing others, and with empathy, we become encouraging—that is, we give others courage. This is the great sum of embracing and empathy.

And each of the character traits noted combine to create authenticity. They are each a greater whole than the sum of the attitudes on the inside and the behaviors we display.

It stands to reason that if we want to be regarded as authentic, lawful, truthful, responsible, unifying, as having integrity, sensible, mature and encouraging that we would have to work toward these. Certainly, we may be able to display these in a several areas of our lives, but it is in the areas where there are challenges, and obstacles that displaying these can help us. And to display them takes work. If you don't believe it then ask yourself would there be disharmony if a person did each of the traits in the list of attitudes, behaviors, and character traits? Many people would recognize that likely there would be greater harmony and less harmful behavior if more people exhibited those traits.

And yet, many of us would also recognize that studying and learning to demonstrate these traits cannot be all that is necessary to bring about harmony. Could there be more?

21

The World System, Universal Principles

Behavior	System
Active	Acts
Loving	Laws
Thoughtful	Technology
Responsive	Rights
Uniting	Unity
Individualizing	Individualism
Sensitive	Social sensibility
Meaningful	Markets
Empathy	Environment

CREATING HARMONY

Many of us probably recognize by this point that we can do more to create harmony, but also perhaps, throughout have questioned whether the power is within the individual to transform the world into one that is more harmonious. After all, isn't there so much that is out of our control? For example, the system seems to have a life of its own. Politicians, policy makers, business leaders, philanthropists, investors, the media, aren't these the ones who really cause or prevent many of the harms based on the decisions they make?

Laws may be crafted in such a way as to fall short in preventing harms. Business leaders may act in ways that create harm. Money makes the world go round and many products and services which could bring about more harmony don't get funded, and many products and services which actually cause harm do get funded.

How can an individual who brings these traits into their lives to a greater degree change the overall way things are done by those who control the world—or most of the money?

To answer this, let's consider the possibility that our society is like a human body, too. Much as our individual behavior can be aligned, so too, our collective behavior can be aligned.

What it takes is a recognition that there are various facets of the system which serve distinct purposes for a healthy, aligned society.

Imagine for a moment that the acts of the collective need to be aligned, much as the acts of the individual need to be aligned for harmony to be achieved. And imagine for a moment that the laws of the collective need to be loving, as in pumping or delivering resources in such a way as to deliver life's essentials, liberty, equality and happiness. And imagine that technology needs to play the role of the brain, and that it needs to be used in thoughtful ways.

Our *love*, and *loving* one another, for example, connects to the *laws* we make. How we love one another creates the laws we see. When our love is not just, we create laws that are unjust. When our love is not truly equal, we create a system of laws that doesn't promote equality. Many who know the legal system have seen some innocent left unprotected, and some not innocent left protected. A *truly* loving law, a law based on Love, will be a just law; truth, love and justice are one. Both Martin Luther King, Jr. and Mahatma Gandhi were imprisoned several times for opposing unjust laws. These are obvious and grand examples, but injustice, or unloving laws affect us in everyday ways — people are born into the unwritten laws of an economic system that essentially forces them to engage in work that may not meet with their moral values; people often have to move far from their families to find work; they may be excluded from opportunities to work in careers of their choosing, merely because of "economic ethnicity" — the culture of economics. These are unspoken laws (customs), yet they're very real and strong.

We have unspoken laws within our families, both just and unjust. The unloving laws can play out in a way where people are not always treated equally. By contrast, laws that are based on love, create growth for all.

Beyond written and unwritten "Laws," which are created by, and intended to promote, loving behavior, we have rules, or Rights. Rights, according to one useful description, are a part of a law. A right for example includes the permission to do something and a penalty for doing something you shouldn't do. A person, for example, may have the right to drive on a road, but not to go through a red traffic light.

155

CREATING HARMONY

Actually, what many people don't realize is that people technically are "permitted" to run a red traffic light, but if they do so they risk the penalty of either getting into an accident or receiving a ticket.

When we recognize that our rights are really defined by both what we can or cannot do and by the penalty that may or may not happen or be imposed, [50] we can guide policy makers to change both these elements of rights.

Policy makers, and the people who drive policy makers, can change what a person can or cannot do or they can change the penalty. As an example of changing what people can or cannot do, consider a change made to a car, whereby when you get in the car, the seat belt automatically straps you in. You no longer can easily avoid the seat belt. That's a change in what you can or cannot do, not in the penalty. Of course, you can bypass this by snapping in the belt under you, but assume the car would not start with such a snap. This is a change in what you can or cannot do. Contrast that to the standard approach of trying to influence behavior: changing the penalty. Often, changing what people can or cannot do can be more effective at influencing behavior than changing a penalty. However, there are cases where a change in a penalty can help. Consider how laws which take a license away from those who drive under the influence led fewer people to drink and drive. What also brought down the number of drinking and driving fatalities were campaigns which inspired people to take the keys: "friends don't let friends drive drunk." What you find is that when you make changes to what people can or cannot do, and you make changes to the penalties associated with violating what you cannot do, you are restructuring rights to make them more responsive.

THE WORLD SYSTEM, UNIVERSAL PRINCIPLES

Much as we can craft laws and rights that aim to create more harmonious behavior, we can employ *technology* in *thoughtful* ways to create more harmonious behavior.

We create our world with thought. And technology, and tools, are an extension of our thoughts. When we have loving thoughts, we create technology that represents that love. When we have harmful, selfish and greedy thoughts, we have technology that is representative of these and symbolic of them—as energy follows thought. Everything we see out there is a continuation of us and of where we are continuing to focus our thoughts.

There are many people who are moving toward creating a more loving, more harmonious world. On the one hand, our technology connects us with people far away; we can have the Dalai Lama or other inspirational leaders in our living room, if we choose; their thoughts can guide us to expand our own awareness. On the other hand, our advanced technology can bring violent video games and other dangerous media into homes where children (and adults) are vulnerable. Perhaps, there is a correlation between harmful technologies and their content (thought) and violence in the real world.

When our thoughts become focused on developing tools to bring life's essentials to all the world's people, and on bringing about equality with liberty, and bringing about the opportunity of people to pursue happiness, we are able to take a step forward towards more harmony.

Laws and technology can spread love and thoughtfulness. And love and thoughtfulness can spread laws and technology for the good of all.

As laws, technology, and rights arise in our world through our beautiful behaviors of love, thought and response, so too, arises social sensibility through sensitivity. Social responsibility, a

CREATING HARMONY

conventional term, follows sensitivity. Social responsibility is a movement of loving, thoughtful people being sensitive, then responsive to the environment, human rights and the need for better human relations. Social responsibility, which stems from social sensitivity, includes the innumerous green measures people take. It includes the social justice and civil rights movements.

It also includes consumerism movements, which themselves, generate more meaningful markets. Meaningful markets are those which aim to make more just and harmonious products and services.

Loving laws, thoughtful technology, meaningful markets, and social sensibility all interact with each other. When we move into harmony with ourselves and others in our behaviors and actions we affect our system. When we become more loving, uniting and responsive, we will begin creating laws and forming new companies that are reflective of this. We will begin creating new ideas based on a shared responsibility and commitment to delivering happiness, equality, freedom and life's essentials to all.

We can change the world on massive levels. As we move into harmony in our own lives, we create more harmony on a global level. Working on ourselves, self-reflecting, in our relationships and interactions with our families, co-workers and friends, we can cultivate more right, loving, thoughtful action. We can all be a part of creating change in the world.

22

The World System - Uniting and the Individual

Behavior	System
Active	Acts
Loving	Laws
Thoughtful	Technology
Responsive	Rights
Uniting	**Unity**
Individualizing	**Individualism**
Sensitive	Social sensibility
Meaningful	Markets
Empathy	Environment

THE WORLD SYSTEM: UNITING AND THE INDIVIDUAL

Uniting and the Individual

In the system, beyond our laws, rights, markets and technology, we have unity and individualism. These two are similar to our uniting and individualizing behaviors in our lives.

Unity and individualism are two forces or parts to a balanced whole. Both are forces that define our world. Of course, these two forces are at odds with certain parts of the world, such as the West, championing individualism, and other parts of the world, the East, championing community, but we should be aware that the two are at work in the West, and we are seeing Eastern countries becoming more individualistic.

For those who think of the United States as a highly individualistic country, recognize, too, the United States, itself, is a unity. And "we, the people" captures the idea of a unity as well.[51] E.J. Dionne makes this point in a PBS Newshour interview with Judy Woodruff:

> Well, I argue that from the beginning, Americans have been torn by a deep, but I think ultimately healthy tension between our love of individualism and liberty on the one side and our love for and quest for community on the other side.
>
> And I think this goes all the way back to the Puritan founding when John Winthrop talked about how we must identify with each other and labor and suffer together and celebrate together. And this communitarian side of us, this part of that emphasizes the common good tends not to be emphasized a lot.
>
> We tend to look at ourselves as a country that's basically about individual freedom and liberty. And I

don't deny for an instant that individual freedom and liberty is very important to us.

But I think that, from the beginning, we have understood that only if we acted together, only if we came to the defense of each other's liberty, does the system work.

One of the great facts is the first word of our Constitution is the word "we." I think we often forget that, "We the people of the United States," not the persons of the United States, but the people. We are a group, as well as a set of individuals with rights that we cherish.

Another way to conceive of the tension between unity and individualism is in terms of cooperation and community. Cooperation and community are ways of speaking of unity. Competition is another way of speaking of the value of the individual.[52] Though we may think of these as either or propositions, we ought to recognize that the two can be harmonized, and in fact, harmonizing them is essential for creating more harmonious interactions and relationships. A good example that makes the point is sports, where teamwork and individual contribution work together, balancing each other. Another example is in the corporate or organizational world where individuals unite for the purpose of the overall group, or unit.

And so what we see is that nature, or harmonizing, is balancing tensions, or opposing forces.

Unity promotes the group over the individual and individualism promotes the individual over the group. Since these seemingly opposing forces are so prevalent in our daily lives, should it not surprise us, also, that the broader world is divided into an East and a West, one of which champions Unity and the other Individualism? Are they not balancing each other? But should we not also be heartened by the fact that each are becoming more of a blend themselves? Are the two not becoming more alike, with the East adopting some Western ways and the West adopting some Eastern?

The sooner we recognize and embrace the reality that these two dynamics are strong forces in the world, which are not going away, the sooner we will put them both better to work for us (harmonize them) in our companies and activities, and thereby create more peace and harmony.

Though we think of these two forces as competing, in fact, they are harmonizing, in the sense that this East-West tension creates a balance.

And, balance will continue to play out in other realms, the political for example. Much as the East and the West each champion unity and individualism, to different degrees, the same is true of the Democrats and Republicans. Democrats tend to favor unity. One need only go to Democrats.com and see its banner heading, "Unity," or to the various "unity" rallies of the Democrat Party to see the value they've placed on the concept. Republicans tend to favor individualism. One need only do an internet search of "individualism and conservatism" to see that. The world is growing and evolving with these two forces placing a "check" on one another — in fact, the framers of the Constitution believed in "checks and balances" of these two forces. The whole effort of the Constitution was to protect the rights of the individual from the government, while putting in place a government to create a unity (United States).

CREATING HARMONY

Putting it all together

So unity and individuality need to be harmonized. And to do this we use our love, thought, response, sensitivity, meaning and empathy. We shape markets, technology (and tools),[53] social responsibility, the environment, laws and rights to balance our individual and group objectives. It seems to be the nature of things that our self-interest and our interest in others are in tension, and either being harmonized poorly or well by us.

We create a balanced system when we act individually in harmony with our self's purpose and the purpose of the whole.

There is evidence of individual and group progress, but also of decline. Measured in terms of population growth, we might say that the species is surviving, even thriving—for now. We are individuals who, by and large, get along (unity) to the point of multiplying our species, from about 800 million, only 250 years ago, to over seven billion today (individuals). Despite our problems, we are still growing. But—and it is a big but—maybe we are growing too fast (or consuming too much, or in a misaligned way). Nearly every major ecosystem is in decline![54]

When we think about harmonizing we can recognize that the environment must be considered a part of harmonizing, after all, we cannot survive without it.

When we recognize that these five, markets, technology, rights, laws, and social sensibility, have worked together to enable us to get along and survive, but that every one of these is also contributing to the declines in the ecosystems, we realize how important it is that we harmonize our lives. We realize that we are being called to create loving laws, use technology thoughtfully, respond to one another rightly, be socially sensitive, develop our markets more meaningfully, and empathize with our environment, and all those who live in it.

THE WORLD SYSTEM: UNITING AND THE INDIVIDUAL

It is as if there is a law of nature where we can bring, through our thoughtful, loving acts, our mind, body and soul, these several defining characteristics of our world (markets, laws, rights, unity, individualism, environment) together in an orderly or *organ*ized way for harmony.

These are defining characteristics of the world. After all, one cannot escape that there is an environment, we make tools and technology, we create rules, laws (whether government or familial), we are social animals (sensitive, to varying degrees), and we have markets—we trade with one another.

Each of these is inescapable, so how we use them is what matters. One can either bring virtuous behaviors to the markets and technology, aligning themselves with nature to go with its grain, or one can work against the grain. All our efforts are more successful when we run with the grain of nature.

In the effort to harmonize self with others, individualism with unity, we can engage our environment in a more socially responsible, or sensitive way, a way that leads to crafting rights which are responsive to our shared needs. We can develop and employ tools and technology in more thoughtful ways. We can connect our actions and decisions to caring about the world with recognition of our role and responsibility.

When we, individually, connect our cares and our thoughts to our shared needs, we inevitably craft rights, create technology, and design laws which deliver upon the ideals we hold that all are created equal and have the right to life, liberty and the pursuit of happiness.

23

A Formula or Recipe?

A FORMULA OR A RECIPE?

The approach of this book could be taken by some people to be offering a recipe or formula for harmonious behavior. Nothing could be further from the truth. A formula is rigid and linear, one plus one equals two. What this book is suggesting is that general concepts and a general analogy is a useful way to broaden our understanding of nature and of our actions.

Much as we use categorical terms to classify a variety of things from animals to our spending (budgets) or organization of our workplaces (departments), we can use categorical terms to understand our actions.

Without an anchor, here, the human body, for such an approach, one person's list is going to differ from another's. In other words, one person may prefer *friendship* or *caring* over *love*, as a pinnacle concept. We use love because it has been universally and intuitively correlated with the heart for millennia.

Further, we offer concepts that might be reasonably related, such as the senses with sensitivity. Besides the relationship between the roots of the words, there is a case to be made that we can learn more about how to be sensitive by engaging our senses in being sensitive, sensitivity defined as: "endowed with sensation; having perception through the senses," and as "having acute mental or emotional sensibility; aware of and responsive to the feelings of others," to take one definition.[55] Note the close correlation between the senses and sensitivity in the definition. Note, also, the close correlation between sensitive and responsiveness in that definition. We can make the case that sensitive and responsive are connected like senses and nerves.

Similarly, we can see the relationship between responding and being responsive, with one definition of responsive: "responding, especially readily and sympathetically to appeals, efforts, influences, etc.: a responsive government."[56] It is basic science that our nerves respond. Thus, the close relationship between the function of the nerves and the function of being responsive.

Beyond the basic correlation between the behaviors we've covered and parts of the body, the claim could be made that there are far more behaviors related to behaving lovingly. Of course, that is true, as is the fact that there are far more body parts in the body. It's a simple matter to extend the analogy out further to draw additional parallels between other behaviors and other body parts—something the authors have done in other writings.

Beyond extending the analogy out vertically (that is, by listing more behaviors), there is a case to be made for a broader understanding of the "spheres" in which we might identify traits. The ABCs are an example of a horizontal development, that is, Attitude, Behavior and Character broaden our look horizontally. We can go further, horizontally, and look at our societal structure in terms of the body analogy, something we have done too (as did Plato, Hobbes, Spencer and numerous others) when we looked at laws, technology and tools, and so on.

The point is, this is completely non-linear and non-formulaic. Much as the body, including the brain, is not completely understood, so too, our behavior, and the interrelations between behaviors, is far more complex than we are able to understand.

It is hard to imagine that if there is some underlying order to creating harmonious interactions it has not been discovered until now. Perhaps it has been discovered numerous times before by unknown, even countless, people. One wonders what it will take for it to be as common knowledge as that the earth revolves around the sun.

We urge you, if you have read to this point, to encourage someone else to read this. If it is true that much more harmony could be created by widespread understanding and use of this approach, then you can be part of bringing a revolutionary, or resolutionary, change to the world.

We, the authors, can attest to the fact that the approach has been helpful to us in creating more harmony. But as with any approach, it must be used by someone for it to work for them. What we urge you to do is memorize some of the words. And begin to see if in becoming more thoughtful, more responsive, more sensitive, and so on, things improve. If they do, then go deeper into learning about them. And to do so, share them with someone you love, as it is in the sharing that the most growth can occur.

24

Growth in Our Society

GROWTH IN OUR SOCIETY

Could this approach, this discovery, utilized by people, open the way to a new era, a way of harmonizing our world? And could it set in motion harmonious growth in our society, whereby we achieve amazing strides and progress with less "creative *destruction*" and turmoil?

Interestingly, the idea that we could improve our lives and the world by better understanding a comparison of the functions of body parts to the function of behaviors happens to be an idea which has historical precedence. It builds upon the two dominant metaphors of the last few hundred years: the Enlightenment Machine Metaphor and the Computer Metaphor. Those two metaphors have been instrumental in the way our society and world has developed, and in the way we interact.

One, the Machine Metaphor

Many attribute the age of reason, also known as the Enlightenment, or the age of Enlightenment, whereby science and reason became the dominating forces, as being based upon a simple metaphor. As science and philosophy writer, Zainab Goonay describes it, "From the seventeenth to the nineteenth centuries, the dominant metaphor was the machine metaphor: The world is a machine. This connection was made by Galileo (d. 1642), Descartes (d. 1650), Boyle (d. 1691), and Newton (d. 1727). They imagined the universe as a static, predictable machine."[57] So much did the way they looked at the world affect the world that: "This worldview influenced our beliefs and psyche, as well as the way scientists, philosophers, and other intellectuals thought."[58] It colored the way that society developed. "Scientists started to think of everything in terms of a machine. Muscles were considered to be force-generating machines, nerves to be electronic machines, and photosynthesis to be a solar-powered machine. Lord Kelvin (d. 1907) characterized the universe as a galactic heat engine."[59]

Of course, nothing about that metaphor led to dramatically more harmony. Consider, over the last few centuries, the wars, the deaths, the poverty, the impacts of business and industry, and consumption on the environment, to name only a handful of consequences. Perhaps there were also good consequences from the growth, and age of Enlightenment, not all bad consequences, but, nonetheless, it left a lot in the area of harmony, wholeness and alignment to be desired.

The machine metaphor also had implications for human behavior and belief regarding spirituality. "With the picture of a perfect world-machine, belief in a Creator became a logical necessity, since the machine implies an engineer."[60] The difference between the Enlightenment view and this alignment analogy is that this analogy is saying, it is not necessarily that a Creator has set in motion all things, and it is not that the world is mechanistic, but rather that the blueprint of the body is something we can use to grow more meaningfully, more thoughtfully, more lovingly, whether or not there was, or is, a Creator.

It's not mechanistic, it's organic. We set in motion the cars we see through what we design from our heart, our head, our muscle, and by extension from our love, from our thought and what we find meaningful.

So, we can create a more harmonious world with a better understanding of what it means to align ourselves, and to align with others, or to harmonize. The mechanistic perspective of the age of Enlightenment viewed the possibility that the universe ran on principles of mechanics similar to those of a watch — gears coming together, etc.[61] That led them to place a priority on the issue of whether there was a designer, a maker—and it led to a thought among many that the world had been wound up like a watch, set to tick, automatically in a predetermined way. It led them to think we could understand the world as we understand a machine, through science. But they didn't stop to ask, what was the behavioral analog to pumping? To responding? Sure gears respond, but was there a behavioral analog? Did *responsiveness* matter? Was it valuable to human behavior? Did *being loving* matter? They determined that intellect, science and reason mattered more than the heart and love.

Why can't we build our behavior, our world on loving principles, with thoughtfulness, meaningfulness, sensitivity, uniting, individuality, etc. all coming together for wholeness? In some ways, this is very consistent with a machine metaphor, but it goes well beyond because it likens the behavioral and values sphere to, perhaps, the greatest machine, the human body — something far more than a machine, and, thus, far more than a mechanistic view.

Two, the Computer Metaphor

Now, let's move to the next historical metaphor, as described by Goonay, "The computer, the current dominant machine, has become the modern era's dominant metaphor. Visionary physicist Edward Fredkin characterizes the universe as a cosmological computer. The universe appears as a network of a dynamic whole, whose parts are essentially interrelated.... The universe is no longer seen as a simple mechanical machine, but as a more complex high-tech computer system."[62] But notice this metaphor is heavily focused on the brain, since the computer is often compared to the brain, acting as a processor, with memory and storage. One wonders where is the heart, where is the pump for resources to flow throughout the body? Even the car has a pump for fuel, and a pump for water, like a heart connected to a circulatory system. Only the brain, only the computer? Hmmm.

Granted, "[t]he computer metaphor supports the view of a dynamic universe more than Newton's static universe."[63] But the analogy to the body takes it a step further, it's an evolution. "Biologists describe evolution as a movement toward increasing order and complexity."[64] When we begin to see that our behavior — all our behavior — and our values can be categorized under headings, such as sensitivity, like senses; meaningfulness, like muscles; thoughtfulness, like brain, all connected to the heart for love, we realize that, like "all the world is a stage," "all the behaviors and values we live by are a body" — not literally, but metaphorically. We can make our actions, and the world, healthier by becoming more thoughtful, more sensitive, more meaningful....

21ˢᵗ Century: The Body Metaphor

Thus, we suggest that the body metaphor offers us a way to understand human behavior and interactions. By comparing an action to the body, and discerning parts of an aligned action, we can more readily create aligned actions, actions which balance our own individual needs and rights with those of others.

It is similar to the machine metaphor, as we have said, because it recognizes that parts can come together for operation. But again it goes well beyond the machine metaphor because it's not trying to explain the workings of the universe, but rather the workings of harmonious and fulfilling human interactions. And it is similar to the computer metaphor, in that it is quite dynamic.

GROWTH IN OUR SOCIETY

But it goes well beyond the computer metaphor in suggesting that there is a lot more than simply brainpower and thinking that defines the human experience.

Conclusion

"As human beings, our greatness lies not so much in being able to remake the world ... as in being able to remake ourselves."

- Mahatma Gandhi

CONCLUSION

We have control over the life we live. We have a say in the actions we take and the choices we make. And so, we have a say in who we are, what we do and who we become.

And since our choices and actions affect others, we have a say in what others do and how they feel.

By extension, we have a say in changing ourselves, and also changing others. By making more balanced, our cares, thoughts, responses, how we unite, how we express our individuality, what we are sensitive to, the difference we make, and the emotional empathy we offer, we create more alignment with others.

We are each beautiful. So, we can make our actions, our lives and our world beautiful. We can achieve happiness, equality, freedom and life's essentials for one and all.

With an understanding that nothing outside changes without each of us changing first on the inside, we begin to create change within ourselves. Is it not true that we, in fact, are a part of the aligned or misaligned institutions (e.g., government, businesses) and activities that we see? Of course, it is. What exists "out there" began within each of us, with thought, centuries of accumulated individual and collective thought. And as energy and movement follow thought, we create the world we see, each and every day. Together and individually, we each make a difference. We can each add more balance and harmony, or we can each add to the separation, inequality and imbalance. It's our choice, each day, and in every way.

Choosing harmony for ourselves and others begins with striving to know who we are and it begins with striving to be what we can fully be. We are our acts. By connecting to the love in our hearts and the "light" of our minds, we begin to act with more balance. By engaging ourselves with the meaning of happiness, and by using our freedom wisely, we grow. We see that we are equal. And ultimately, the earth begins to blossom as life's essentials are "allowed" and made to flow to all.

CREATING HARMONY

With love, thoughtfulness and responsiveness, we act with heart, mind and courage. With sensitivity and empathy, we act with our senses and emotions in check, honoring feelings and extending our care. With unity and individuality, we act flexibly and supportive. Joined in harmony, together, we act whole, balanced, aligned and altruistically.

It is up to us. We can't change the world without changing ourselves. The task is great, but so are we. It's within our power to speak and move in a myriad of ways, acting aligned with one another.

NOTES

NOTES

[1] Fact Monster, http://www.factmonster.com/analogies?opt=showhint Sep. 8, 2012, Analogy of the Day.

[2] Interactions and relationships are part of processes. The assertion being made is that each of these functions, such as responding, linking, thinking are part of every natural human process.

[3] This is a point also made in *The Anatomy of Our Behavior*, Cathy LoGerfo and Christopher Dunn.

[4] The Guardian, Rolf Dobelli, Friday 12 April 2013 15.00 EDT, http://www.theguardian.com/media/2013/apr/12/news-is-bad-rolf-dobelli

[5] Id.

[6] Id.

[7] Id.

[8] See e.g., Psychology Today, How To Love Yourself First, The least-honored--and most powerful path to self-love, Post published by Ken Page L.C.S.W. on May 21, 2011 in Finding Love

[9] https://www.google.com/?gws_rd=ssl#q=define:+responsive

[10] http://en.wikipedia.org/wiki/Golden_mean_(philosophy)

[11] http://en.wikipedia.org/wiki/Golden_mean_(philosophy)

[12] http://en.wikipedia.org/wiki/Golden_mean_(philosophy)

[13] This is a point also made in *The Anatomy of Our Behavior*, Cathy LoGerfo and Christopher Dunn.

[14] Id.

[15] The Telegraph, The animals and plants we cannot live without, By Richard Gray, Science Correspondent 2:12PM GMT 15 Nov 2008, http://www.telegraph.co.uk/news/earth/wildlife/3463912/The-animals-and-plants-we-cannot-live-without.html

[16] This is a point also made in *The Anatomy of Our Behavior*, Cathy LoGerfo and Christopher Dunn.

[17] Id.

[18] Id.

[19] Id.

[20] Oxford American Writer's Thesaurus, 561.

[21] This is a point also made in *The Anatomy of Our Behavior*, Cathy LoGerfo and Christopher Dunn.

---

[22] The amygdala in the emotion-generating limbic system is where feelings of empathy are believed to be generated. See e.g., What Can Neuroscience Tell Us about Evil? Richard Brandt on April 24, 2007, available at http://www.technologyreview.com/news/407738/what-can-neuroscience-tell-us-about-evil/

[23] This is a point also made in *The Anatomy of Our Behavior*, Cathy LoGerfo and Christopher Dunn.

[24] See e.g., http://www.collinsdictionary.com/dictionary/english/happy

[25] Enzymes are proteins that catalyze reactions, for example, breaking down food. Without enzymes, simple things like digesting foods, would be impossible. For example, people who are lactose intolerant cannot break down milk because they lack the necessary enzyme to do so. See e.g., Wikihow.com, *How are enzymes important in living things?* Available at http://wiki.answers.com/Q/How_are_enzymes_important_in_living_things

[26] http://en.wikipedia.org/wiki/Enzyme (citing Jaeger KE, Eggert T.; Eggert (2004). "Enantioselective biocatalysis optimized by directed evolution". Current Opinion in Biotechnology 15 (4): 305–13).

[27] The Ten Happiest Countries in the World and Why We're Not One of Them, http://www.fastcoexist.com/3017037/the-10-happiest-countries-in-the-world-and-why-were-not-one-of-them

[28] See e.g., The Background of Gross National Happiness, http://www.gnhbhutan.org/about/The_background_of_Gross_National_Happiness.aspx

[29] http://www.un.org/en/documents/udhr/

[30] https://www.google.com/#q=define:+mercy

[31] The Dalai Lama notes that "a gut-level recognition of the fundamental equality of self and others as human beings [is necessary to those] who aspire to happiness and wish to avoid suffering." *Id.* at 172 (2011).

[32] The idea to counter the "numbness of the heart" is a twist on Smith's idea of countering, with education, the "numbness of the mind" that came with division of labor. Legal scholar Robin Paul Malloy notes, of Adam Smith: "He was of the view that a basic education would help offset the 'numbness of the mind' and consequent alienation that would occur to the many labouring poor. He notes in his argument that the poor should be given such an education precisely because they cannot afford it and even if the sole beneficiaries of the education were the individuals themselves. There was no need to show a benefit to society that would outweigh the cost of such a program. Smith's concern was not one of utilitarianism or wealth maximization. He was

concerned with the individual." Robin Paul Malloy, Adam Smith and the Modern Discourse of Law and Economics, in ADAM SMITH AND THE PHILOSOPHY OF LAW AND ECONOMICS 120 (Robin P. Malloy & Jerry Evensky eds., 1994).

[33] *Id.*

[34] See e.g., The Guardian, Spain youth unemployment reaches record 56.1%, at http://www.theguardian.com/business/2013/aug/30/spain-youth-unemployment-record-high

[35] See e.g., Environmental Working Group, McDonald's Makes The Switch From Foam To Paper Hot Cups, at http://www.ewg.org/enviroblog/2013/09/mcdonald-s-makes-switch-foam-paper-hot-cups The group notes the harms: "Studies have found that workers in plants that manufacture styrene, which is used to make polystyrene, have experienced central nervous system problems that include headache fatigue, dizziness, confusion, drowsiness, malaise, difficulty in concentrating and a feeling of intoxication. The International Agency for Research on Cancer classifies styrene a known carcinogen. In addition, products made from polystyrene foam do not easily biodegrade, persist in landfills for centuries and are a major polluter of the oceans, where they break down into small pieces and kill many birds and fish that mistake them for food. Polystyrene is banned or restricted in food packaging in many cities, towns and counties in California and across the nation, including Seattle and Brookline and Amherst, Mass. Paper cups break down faster and can be recycled, making them a much more sustainable option."

[36] Merriam-Webster Dictionary, at http://www.merriam-webster.com/dictionary/attune

[37] http://www.thank-your-stars.com/stories-about-janitors.html

[38] https://www.google.com/webhp?sourceid=chrome-instant&ion=1&espv=2&ie=UTF-8#sourceid=chrome-psyapi2&ie=UTF-8&q=define%3A%20respect

[39] Stories for preaching.com, Understanding Others, citing "Scientific information adapted from *When Elephants Weep." When Elephants Weep,* by Jeffrey Moussaieff Masson. http://storiesforpreaching.com/category/sermonillustrations/understanding-others/

[40] Id.

[41] http://www.merriam-webster.com/dictionary/sympathy

[42] Id.

[43] See e.g., Stanford Encyclopedia of Philosophy, Hume's Moral Philosophy
http://plato.stanford.edu/entries/hume-moral/
[44] The Meaning of Mutuality, Judith V. Jordan, Phd.,1, 1986,
http://www.wellesleycentersforwomen.com/pdf/previews/preview_23sc.pdf
[45] Id.
[46] http://www.merriam-webster.com/dictionary/authentic
[47] See e.g., Lincoln's Honesty, by Gordon Leidner of Great American History,
available at http://www.greatamericanhistory.net/honesty.htm
[48] https://www.google.com/#q=define:+integrity
[49] Character Counts in Iowa, A very special seed – a story about integrity,
Posted on Feb 22, 2013, at
http://www.charactercountsiniowa.org/2013/02/22/a-very-special-seed-a-story-about-integrity/#.VLg3mivF-So
[50] For a more thorough consideration of rights, see Christopher Dunn,
Clarifying the View of the Cathedral: The Four Dimensions of the Framework and the Calabresi Theorem, Bocconi University Law Review, available at
www.bocconilegalpapers.org/wp-content/uploads/.../BLP-2011-04-EN.pdf.
[51] E.J. Dionne makes this point in an PBS Newshour interview with Judy
Woodruff:

> Well, I argue that from the beginning, Americans have been torn by a deep, but I think ultimately healthy tension between our love of individualism and liberty on the one side and our love for and quest for community on the other side.
>
> And I think this goes all the way back to the Puritan founding when John Winthrop talked about how we must identify with each other and labor and suffer together and celebrate together. And this communitarian side of us, this part of that emphasizes the common good tends not to be emphasized a lot.
>
> We tend to look at ourselves as a country that's basically about individual freedom and liberty. And I don't deny for an instant that individual freedom and liberty is very important to us.
>
> But I think that, from the beginning, we have understood that only if we acted together, only if we came to the defense of each other's liberty, does the system work.
>
> One of the great facts is the first word of our Constitution is the word "we." I think we often forget that, "We the people of the United States," not the persons of the United States, but the people.

NOTES

We are a group, as well as a set of individuals with rights that we cherish.

Available at http://www.pbs.org/newshour/bb/politics/july-dec12/dionne_08-20.html, air date August 20, 2012

[52] This is similar to Herbert Spencer's "survival of the fittest" philosophy and Social Darwinism.

[53] Tools is a more general and encompassing term, because it goes beyond our modern day usage of the word technology.

[54] The Millennium Ecosystem Assessment available at www.maweb.org/. "Prepared by more than 1,300 experts from 95 countries, the report 'shows how human activities are causing environmental damage on a massive scale throughout the world and how biodiversity--the very basis for life on Earth--is declining at an alarming rate,' UN Secretary General Kofi Annan said in a statement. The assessment cost $22 million and was supported by the UN, the World Bank, and foundations." *Ecosystems In Decline, UN Finds, Report says global ecological damage threatens efforts to eradicate poverty*, Bette Hileman, Chemical and Engineering News, available at www.pubs.acs.org. *See also,*
BBC Report, *Study highlights global decline,* by Jonathan Amos, March 30, 2005, available at http://news.bbc.co.uk/2/hi/science/nature/4391835.stm.

[55] Dictionary.com, at http://dictionary.reference.com/browse/sensitive

[56] Dictionary.com, at http://dictionary.reference.com/browse/responsive

[57] Metaphors in Science, Zainab Goonay, Issue 40, Oct. – Dec. 2002 at http://www.fountainmagazine.com/Issue/detail/Metaphors-in-Science.

[58] Id.

[59] Id.

[60] Id.

[61] See e.g., Descartes, The World and Other Writings, Treatise on Man, 169, Stephen Gaukroger ed., Cambridge University Press (2004).

[62] Metaphors in Science, Zainab Goonay, Issue 40, Oct. – Dec. 2002 at http://www.fountainmagazine.com/Issue/detail/Metaphors-in-Science.

[63] Id.

[64] Id.

Proof

Made in the USA
Charleston, SC
07 December 2015